Passing through ...

my History

Mishie's Memories

my Life

the Hatting

a collection of reminiscences,
facts and information
that has surrounded
my being ...

Tony Stafford

Passing through ...

This edition first published by Tony Stafford
Scrumpy Cottage, Buttercombe Barton
West Down, Devon EX34 8NU

copyright © Tony Stafford 2015

ISBN-13: 978-1508644040

my History

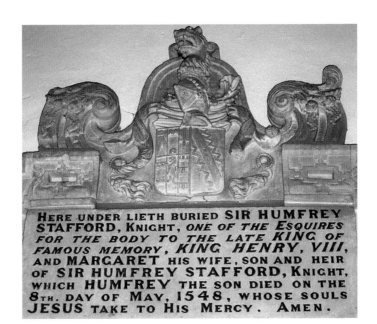

HERE UNDER LIETH BURIED SIR HUMFREY STAFFORD, KNIGHT, ONE OF THE ESQUIRES FOR THE BODY TO THE LATE KING OF FAMOUS MEMORY, KING HENRY, VIII, AND MARGARET HIS WIFE, SON AND HEIR OF SIR HUMFREY STAFFORD, KNIGHT, WHICH HUMFREY THE SON DIED ON THE 8TH. DAY OF MAY, 1548, WHOSE SOULS JESUS TAKE TO HIS MERCY. AMEN.

Introduction

It is, of course, extremely egotistical for me to call this small chapter "My History".

I am but one of thousands of characters who inhabit the genealogy of the Stafford and Walton families. For those of you, related to me, who read it – it is, naturally, your history too.

The marvel of DNA technology now allows scientists to assert quite definitely from where and from whom we are descended. It is said that 70% of the English population have genes inherited from Attila the Hun; whilst perhaps the other 30% comes from a blue eyed Danish princess. In truth, it is likely we have all arrived from a singular point.

The particular significance of the Stafford name is that, as far as we know, all so named are descended from a Norman Knight after 1066. Wherever I go abroad, I take a perverse delight in looking for Stafford's in the local phone directory and I have never been disappointed! Our American cousins are peculiarly addicted to family history, and some of their genealogies seem to encompass every Monarch, Prelate and Famous name known to man.

In this history, I have tried to be as realistic and accurate as possible. It helps, of course, having a great name – perhaps one of the grandest in English medieval history. But even so, there can still be pitfalls, omissions and inaccuracies in the journals and family records I have researched.

I hope "My History" will help you understand where you fit into this extraordinary scheme, and that you may share the pathos, interest, humour and joy of our ancestors with our future generations.

Tony Stafford, June 2008

"I have inside me blood of kings ... "[1]

1066 and all that

As we all know, on the 14th October 1066, Duke William of Normandy defeated King Harold II at the Battle of Hastings and thus became the next King of England – William I, the Conqueror.

One of his trusted companions, and holding the favoured position of standard bearer, was his cousin Ralph de Tosny, Count of Evreux and Seigneur[2] of Conches. He was accompanied by his younger brothers, Robert and Nigel. At the time of the invasion Robert was 31 years old and had been recently bereaved during the previous year; when his young wife, Avice de Clare, had died giving birth to his first son, Nicholas.

Robert's family had been Barons of Tosny[3], a small village on the River Seine situated some 100 kilometres north west of Paris; since Hugh de Cavalcamp (born c. 890) had established their fiefdom there. Hugh was the son of Haldrick Eysteinsson[4] of Maer in Norway and Maud, daughter of Baldwin II (known funnily enough as "the Bald"), Count of Flanders and Lady Alfrith (or Elfrida), daughter of King Alfred the Great[5].

Following the Conquest, the favoured Companions were given considerable land holdings in England. By the time of the Domesday Book, complied in 1086; Robert had accumulated a great fiefdom that tended into seven counties, including that of the town of Stafford[6]; from which he took his name and so created the great and influential Stafford dynasty.

---

[1] or as my wife says - one small drip
[2] Akin to an English Lord
[3] Sometimes spelt Tosnii or Tonei
[4] The male ancestry can be traced back through various chiefs and Kings of Norway, Denmark and Sweden to Radbart, King of Gardarige c. 600 AD
[5] My 34th Great grandfather
[6] see endnotes

The Stafford Knot and the Dukes of Buckingham

After Robert died in 1088, his son, Nicholas, continued the building of both the great castle[7] at Stafford and the family fortune. His son, Robert, fathered only a daughter, Millicent; and her husband, Hervey Bagot, a tenant and junior knight, succeeded to the fiefdom in her right (1194): their descendant, Edmund de Stafford (having assumed the surname), was summoned to the court as a baron by Edward I in 1299. Edmunds son, Ralph, a warrior like his father, became famous in the French wars when he conducted the brilliant defence of Aiguillon against the armies of France, fought at Crecy and again took part in the siege of Calais. He was chosen as a Knight of the Garter at the foundation of the order[8] and he was further created Earl of Stafford in 1351.

His son Hugh, who succeeded as 2nd Earl in 1372, also served in the French wars. From 1376 he became prominent in politics, probably through his marriage to a daughter of the Earl of Warwick, and was one of the four lords on the committee in the Good Parliament. He also served on the 'continual councils' that from 1378 to 1380 looked after the interests of the ten year old Richard II. He was friendly, however, with that king, and was with him on his Scottish expedition in 1385. He died the next year at Rhodes on a pilgrimage to the Holy Land. The marriage of his son, Thomas, the 3rd Earl, in 1392, to Anne of Gloucester, the daughter and eventual heiress of Thomas, Duke of Buckingham (son of Edward III), and also a joint heiress of the great house of Bohun[9], proved a decisive turning-point in the history of the Stafford's. Although he died childless, this great lady[10] married in 1398 his brother Edmund, the 5th Earl, who obtained, in addition to her great possessions, her ancestors' office of Lord High Constable in 1403. Unfortunately for him, he was killed the same year at the Battle of Shrewsbury, commanding the van of the king's army. Their son, Humphrey (1402-1460), the first Stafford duke of Buckingham, was thus placed by his descent and possessions in the front rank of the English nobility.

By 1483, the Stafford's had become so powerful that they aroused the jealousy of the King, Richard III. Henry the 2nd Duke had become

---

[7] In fact, there were two castles at Stafford. The "family" building was constructed outside the original town.

[8] He became one of the twenty-six founding members and the fifth Knight - his banner is still displayed in St George's Chapel at Windsor Castle

[9] The Earldom of Hereford

[10] In her will she was styled "Countess of Stafford, Buckingham, Hereford and Northampton"

involved in a plot[11] to depose the King, and was tried for treason. His estates were attaindered[12], but were completely restored after the defeat and death of Richard III by Henry Tudor (Henry VII) at the Battle of Bosworth[13] in 1485, when Edward, the 3rd duke (1478-1521), regained the title and estates.

During the reign of Henry VIII, his great position, fortified by his relationship to the Percy's, Howards and Neville's, made him a natural leader of the old nobility, while his recovery of the ancestral office of Lord High Constable in 1509 increased his prestige. However, he had not the sufficient force of character to take an active part in politics, and the king's easily roused suspicions were excited by private accusations in 1521.

After a nominal trial by his peers, he was beheaded on the 17th of May 1521, a subsequent act (1523) confirming his attainder. His 'fate', even under such a king, made a great sensation, exciting sympathy at home, and moving the French Emperor, Charles V, to say "that a butcher's dog (Wolsey) had pulled down the noblest buck in England". It is noteworthy that the 2nd and 3rd Dukes were both beheaded, while the 1st Duke fell in the Wars of the Roses.

Unfortunately, my Stafford heritage did not devolve very far through that great Buckingham family, as our branch is descended from Ralph's younger brother, William, who was born about 1306 in Tunbridge, Staffordshire. He was known as Sir William de Stafford.

Uprisings, killings and beheadings

My 15th great Grandfather, Sir Humphrey Stafford[14], born in 1400, was Lord of the Manor of Grafton in Northamptonshire, and Sheriff of Stafford in the reigns of Henry IV and Henry VI. He was also one of the Knights for the County of Stafford in Parliament and was appointed Governor of Calais.

---

[11] see endnotes

[12] The word "attainder", meaning "taintedness", is part of English common law. Under English law, a criminal condemned for a serious crime, whether treason or felony could be declared "attainted", meaning that his civil rights were nullified: he could no longer own property or pass property to his family by will or testament. His property and any titles would also revert to the Crown. The convicted person would normally be punished by judicial execution as well - when a person committed a capital crime and was put to death for it, the property left behind escheated to the Crown rather than being inherited by family.

[13] The historic site of the Battle is some 6 miles from Witherley, where I was born. New research indicates the possibility that the actual site was very near Atherstone, possibly just across the Watling Street from our former house.

[14] The second cousin of Edmund, 5th Earl Stafford

During the Peasant's revolt of 1450, led by Jack Cade, he was sent by the King to intercept the rebels, who were advancing towards London from where Cade had landed on the Kent coast. Unfortunately General Stafford, rather complacently, thought he could deal with the rabble with only a small force of soldiers; whilst Cade cleverly affecting to be terrified at General Stafford's approach, retreated with his main force to Sevenoaks, but left a strong detachment in ambush to attack Stafford. The Royal Army followed, without observing the necessary caution, and was so furiously attacked by the concealed force that great numbers were cut to pieces. These included Sir Humphrey and allegedly[15], a cousin William Stafford[16], a squire.

Jack Cade continued with his Kentish men on to London, where he murdered a number of notables, mounting their heads on pikes in a ghoulish embrace. The Government alarmed at the great defeat sent his brother, John Stafford, the Archbishop of Canterbury and Humphrey Stafford, Duke of Buckingham to negotiate with the insurgents. Eventually they persuaded the rebels to accept a truce, whilst Cade was abandoned and eventually caught and slain.

Unfortunately, this was not the only tragedy to befall the family. In 1485, the second son, another Humphrey, managed to pick the wrong side to back at the Battle of Bosworth. His support of Richard III was to lead to his execution at Tyburn the following July, and the forfeiture of his estates.

The Stafford's at Blatherwycke

When Sir Humphrey Stafford of Grafton had married Eleanor Aylesbury on 2nd January 1423, she, as the only child of Sir Thomas[17], had already inherited a very large estate which included the Manor of Blatherwycke[18] in Northamptonshire.

Sir Humphrey of Blatherwycke was only eight years old at the time of his father's death, but was already betrothed to Margaret[19], daughter of Sir John Fogge. Sir Humphrey gradually restored the family to royal favour. He eventually received a pardon from Henry VIII, and in 1515 was granted a partial restoration of his land and in 1521 regained the Manor of Milton Keynes. In 1532 he made a settlement of the manor on his further marriage with Joan, widow of William Lane. On his death in 1545, another Humphrey inherited Milton Keynes.

---

[15] *In his play, Henry VI, William Shakespeare refers to the Stafford brothers, but this does not seem to be true.*
[16] *It is quite possible that the William Stafford was his 20 year old illegitimate son.*
[17] *Died 1418*
[18] *Eleanor was born in the Manor in 1407*
[19] *Lady Diana Spencer's 13-Great Grandmother*

Humphrey and Margaret had four sons; the eldest (yet another Humphrey) continued to live at Blatherwycke, became a Squire to Henry VIII and began the building of the great house at Kirby Hall[20] in 1570. However, he never saw it completed as he died in 1575. His younger brother, Sir William of Grafton, married as a young man, Mary Boleyn, the former mistress of the King; who then married her sister, Anne.

Humphrey's second son, John, continued as Lord of Blatherwycke and Huncote. It is assumed he married Bridget Clopton of Kentwall. His death in 1596 is marked by a monument in the small church which still lies next to where the Hall once stood. His son, another John, seems then to have moved to Huncote, located just south of Leicester. Two generations lived here at the Manor until William Stafford (1617 to 1669) who was born at Cosby, another small village just four miles away.

The Leicestershire Farmers

The Stafford's continued to live and presumably work in this village from the mid 17th century through to yet another William (1736 to 1803) who married Elizabeth Warner at St Martin's Church, Leicester on 29th December 1756. At this point they were living at Kirby Bellars, near Melton Mowbray. Sadly, Elizabeth died in childbirth in 1761 at the age of 31. In 1762, he married again to Mary North and had three more children, and after her death in 1794, he married yet again; this time to a Philadelphia Hardy. One must assume at this point that the Stafford wealth of previous times had long since disappeared, as this lady ended up in Leicester Poorhouse in 1827.

Their only surviving child, John, moved around that area of North Leicestershire during his marriage to Elizabeth Ward. Of their seven children, five were born at Twyford, one at Hungarton and the youngest, William, at Thorpe Satchville. At some time after his birth in 1804, his parents moved to Radcliffe Culey, Nr Atherstone.

William, my great, great Grandfather, was originally a cordwainer[21] (shoemaker) and later farmed at Sheepy Magna for 20 years from 1841, and then worked 90 acres at Ratcliffe Culey from 1861. He died in June 1879 having fathered nine children and is buried in the churchyard there. He was the enumerator for the Sheepy Parish in the 1871 census.

---

[20] *Located about 6 miles west of Blatherwycke, roofless, it still stands there today ... a wonderful sight.*

[21] *White's Directory of 1846 confirms his occupation as shoemaker farmer in Sheepy Magna - he also ran the Post Office.*

The Hatters of Atherstone

It was Richard, the youngest of the five sons, who left farming and trained as an accountant. When qualified, he joined the Hat manufacturing company of Hall and Phillips in Atherstone. In December 1872, he established a partnership with William Wilson, who had been the felt manager, and together they started the firm of Wilson and Stafford[22] at Britannia Works by the Coventry canal in Coleshill Road.

At that time Atherstone had a thriving headwear industry with possibly twelve factories specialising in the lower quality wool felt hat market. This was the time of great industrialisation, and therefore high output, hard work, low wages, and eventually exceptional profits for the more ruthless factory managers.

Gradually from small beginnings, they forged the business into the second largest in the town, and bought out smaller factories nearby. At the same time, Richard Stafford became a pillar of Atherstone society, living in a substantial house within walking distance of the factory. He was a member of the Atherstone Board of Guardians, the old Rural Sanitary Authority and became Chairman of the Parish Council; and was very involved in the Atherstone Cricket Club for over fifty years. He and Mary Angrave had five children, of whom the second son, William, was my Grandfather. Their youngest daughter, Annie, was to become the wife of Osborne Vero, and so join the two leading hat manufacturers together by blood, although at that time, never in business[23]!

Will Stafford was the great driving force behind the expansion of the firm. It was under his management that a new three storey building was erected by the canal in the mid thirties and more modern machinery was installed. Apparently he used to stand by the gate through which the employees tramped in the morning to clock-on and closed it exactly on the minute – latecomers had no work or money that day! He would also refuse to see any trade visitors who did not wear a hat!

Will and Maudie Stafford had three children. Dick, the eldest, served in the Second World War as an RAF navigator. Sadly, he died in 1946. Ernest, my father, had already been commissioned into the Territorial Army in the early thirties. He served throughout the war, ending up as a Lieutenant Colonel and Deputy Military Governor for Hanover. In 1946, he rejoined the family business and continued working there until his death in January 1980. Yvonne, the youngest, married and had two children. In 1958, she died very suddenly as a result of a toxic reaction to a bee sting.

---

[22] *started with £100 from his wife*
[23] *Wilson and Stafford eventually took over Vero and Everett Ltd in 1987*

Northern Grit – the Walton story

Our earliest Walton, that we know of so far, is William; born in Durham about 1600 who married Margaret Stoke in 1628. His great grandson Henry, born 1673 married Grace Bateman in 1694 and they settled in the West Allendale area of Northumberland, renting the small farm of Smallburns. After four years they moved locally to Lowturney Shield and then Hearty Cleugh before returning to Smallburns on May Day 1714.

This part of Northumberland is very rugged, with high barren moors and small stone built houses tucked into the sheltered clefts and valleys. Apart from subsistence farming, the main occupation from Roman times was lead mining. Many generations provided labour for this hard and poorly paid work, and it appears that some of the Waltons were mining here from time to time.

Henry Walton died in 1721, leaving three children, of whom the eldest, John, married Mary Lowthian in Kirkoswald Church on 12th September 1728. They had nine children, and the second son, Samuel, at some point, must have taken work over in Cumberland to the west; for in 1775, he married Mary Lazenby. At this time, he was forty-one, whilst she was a girl of eighteen. We do not know what occupation Samuel followed, but coming from a fairly poor family, he must either have done well or inherited from his young wife, for they lived from the start at Geltsdale House. Here they brought up fourteen children, of whom four died in infancy, the youngest born in 1810 and when Samuel was 76!! He died at the good age of 85 with Mary surviving him for a further seventeen years.

Romance at Brackenthwaite

Geltsdale House sits in a wooded valley in the King's Forest of Geltsdale, whilst to the west lies high moorland rising to 1,500 feet before falling away to the valley of the River Eden. There lies a farm called Brackenthwaite, facing west with glorious views of the hills of the Lake District. It was to here that George Walton, the son of Samuel and Mary, used to walk every week over the e fells to court Ann Atkinson. When they married in May, 1819; he was nearly 42, whilst she was ten years younger. They raised five children of whom the fourth, John Atkinson Walton was my great Grandfather.

Brackenthwaite, today, is still, predominantly, a sheep farm; and although the house, itself, is rather plain; the huge old stone barns behind, full of animals at lambing time, is so evocative and so timeless.

It also must have been quite a wealthy farm, for on the map I possess, the land holdings total 1,784 acres[24] in and around Castle Carrock.

John Walton obviously put his farming background to good use, for he eventually was appointed the Land Agent to the Marquis of Exeter, with the responsibility for running the great estate of Burghley House, near Stamford. Eventually, when he retired from that employment, they moved to Lockington, near Derby. Of their nine children, it was the youngest, Thomas[25], born in 1871, who was eventually to inherit the old farm at Brackenthwaite, and to be the most successful of the descendants of Henry Walton.

The Waltons in Derby

Tom Walton was educated at Trent College, and on leaving this well known school, he joined the Westminster Bank. He prospered in this occupation, eventually becoming the manager of the Derby branch. In 1898, he married Ethel Charters of Leicester, and eventually lived at 69 Rose Hill Street, near the famous Arboretum. Their family of four girls and a boy, Peter, were all born here. I remember it well from my childhood. It seemed enormously tall – I think possibly five floors with the attics at the top being a treasure trove of jumble for a young boy! It was set just off the road behind a high brick wall with a small front garden and a Victorian conservatory to the left side.

Tom, at that time in possibly 1950, was a grand old gentleman. Grandmother Walton was a more retiring person, rather grey and sallow, and not particularly well, for she died soon after. Thomas died in 1957 at the age of 86. He had been the Chief Air-raid Warden for Derby during the war; a Governor of Derby High School and was awarded the MBE in 1946.

His great sorrow was that his only son, Peter, was killed in the later stages of the war in August 1944 in a plane crash near Kursa in India. My sadness was that he sold beautiful Brackenthwaite in 1932.

My mother, Muriel, was the youngest of the Walton girls. I think Grandpa Walton had a fairly hard time bringing up four boisterous young ladies, particularly when they matured in the early 1920's. Gwen, being the oldest, was perhaps the most conservative, and I always remember her as being rather stern and austere.

---

[24] *When the Manor House Farm was sold on Saturday, 18th December 1920, 300 acres of mixed arable, pasture and fell land were included with the farm buildings and four cottages. The other land may have been rented or sold since Thomas inherited the farm in 1907*

[25] *Sadly, the two eldest sons died in 1890. George was drowned in the Manawatu River, and buried at Woodville, North Island, New Zealand.*

The other girls, however, were much more of a freer spirit. Judy was the intellectual, and Thea was the party girl. Muriel, being the youngest, probably got away with the most liberty. She was very attached to her younger brother, and was really a tomboy at heart – and so her nickname, amongst her contemporaries, was always "Tommie".

It was Peter, who during the early thirties introduced her to a fellow officer in the Sherwood Foresters; a rather dashing young man with a penchant for fast cars – his name was Ernest Stafford.

meeting one of my distant relatives in 1994
I was Vice Chairman of the Nuneaton Hospital Trust

References and detailed notes

History of Stafford

Legend would have it that the town of Stafford was founded in about 700 AD by a Mercian prince called Bertelin who established a hermitage on a secluded marshy island. The remains of a wooden preaching cross were discovered under the foundations of St Bertelin's Church in the centre of the town. The cross had been laid flat and buried at about the time of the first millennium.

Some two hundred years after St Bertelin, in 913 AD, Aethelflaed, daughter of King Alfred the Great, established the Burgh of Stafford. The town became a frontier post in the Anglo-Saxon's struggle against the Viking Hordes, forming a part of a chain of such timber fortresses including Tamworth and Chester.

Within twenty-five years the town had its own mint (930 - 1156), while the presence of clay led to the establishment of a local pottery industry. Staffordware has been recorded from all over the Midlands.

In the late Saxon period the country was divided into shires. Stafford was chosen as the county town ahead of Tamworth, which had been the capital of the ancient kingdom of Mercia.

Following the Duke of Normandy invasion of England there were a number of rebellions, one of which was led by Edric the Wild and culminated in the battle of Stafford (1069). Two years after the battle Edwin Earl of Mercia was assassinated and his lands distributed amongst William's followers. Robert de Tonei (de Tosny) was granted the manor of Bradley and one third of the king's rents in Stafford.

The king's castle at Stafford was derelict or destroyed by the time the Domesday Book was compiled (1086/7). However, a new castle was constructed by Robert de Tonei some distance away from the troublesome Saxons at Castle Bank. This castle was to become the Family Seat of the Stafford Dynasty.

In 1206 Stafford was granted its Charter of Liberties. This document made Stafford a borough and gave the townspeople the same rights enjoyed in existing boroughs, including the right of inheritance. The Charter remains the cornerstone of the borough's legal existence upon which all other Grants and Charters depend.

During the Middle Ages Stafford became an important market town, dealing particularly in cloth and wool. Meanwhile the lords of Stafford, impoverished as a result of the Crusades in the late twelfth century, flourished once more. Ralph de Stafford was a warrior and served under Edward III during the early phases of the Hundred Years Wars.

Ralph was created Earl of Stafford in 1351, having already been made one of the founder members of the Order of the Garter. The king gave Ralph permission to rebuild his castle at Stafford in 1348, although it would appear that he had already made an agreement with a master mason the year before.

King Richard II visited the town in 1299. He was paraded through the streets as a prisoner by troops loyal to Henry Bolingbroke (the future Henry IV).

From Wikipedia ... In 1483 a conspiracy arose amongst a number of disaffected gentry, supporters of Edward IV. They originally planned to depose Richard III and place Edward V back on the throne. When rumours arose that Edward and his brother (the Princes in the Tower) were dead, Buckingham intervened, proposing instead that Henry Tudor return from exile, take the throne and marry Elizabeth of York. For his part, Buckingham would raise a substantial force from his estates in Wales and the Marches.

By a combination of luck and skill, Richard put down the rebellion: Henry's ships ran into a storm and had to go back to Brittany, and Buckingham's army was greatly troubled by the same storm and deserted when Richard's forces came against them. Buckingham tried to escape in disguise but was turned in for the bounty Richard had put on his head, and he was convicted of treason and beheaded in Salisbury on 2 November. Following Buckingham's execution, his widow, Catherine, married Jasper Tudor.

Jack Cade's rebellion : extract from The Chronicles of England

"John Cade, an Irish refugee, from his resemblance to Sir John Mortimer, of the family of March, who had been irregularly put to death early in this reign, on an accusation of treason, assumed the character of his son; and during the present discontents, A. D. 1450, on the profession of redressing grievances, assembled 20,000 men under his standard in Kent. A force was sent to reduce him under Sir Humphrey Stafford; who being defeated and killed, he encamped on Blackheath; from whence he sent very plausible propositions to the court. T

he gates of the city were obliged to be opened to him; and Cade, who assumed the merit of exact discipline, published severe edicts against all excesses; leading his men out into the fields every night. He sacrificed the treasurer, Lord Say, and Sir James Cromer, the high sheriff of Kent, however, to the fury of his adherents; and the king and council withdrew to Kenelworth.

But as popular insurrections under vulgar leaders seldom preserve that moderation and order, which give permanent success to better-concerted enterprises; Jack Cade and his men could not long bear the power their strength so suddenly procured them. Some merchants had *their houses plundered, particularly two, wherein Cade had been generously entertained; the citizens, therefore, resolved, that when Cade was marched into Southwark, they would shut the gates, and oppose his return. This resolution was communicated to the lord Scales, constable of the Tower of London, and his lieutenant; who greatly encouraged the citizens to persevere in their laudable design: and not only promised them his utmost assistance, but assured them, that, if the rebels should attack the bridge, he would drive them from thence by his artillery in the Tower.*

Cade no sooner understood that he was excluded the city, than he advanced to attack and force his passage over the bridge; but the citizens being prepared to receive him, the drawbridge was obstinately disputed; great numbers of citizens were killed; but, at last, Cade was obliged to retire.

By this gallant defence of the citizens, the rebels were much discouraged; and Cade found himself obliged to recruit his army with the prisoners of the King's-Bench and Marshalsea prisons. But John Stafford, archbishop of Canterbury, and high chancellor, being informed, that the rebels by their bad success in the late engagement were greatly dispirited, wisely improved the opportunity, and, with the bishop of Winchester, immediately drew up an act of indemnity to all who should disperse, giving it the sanction of the great seal. This being proclaimed in Southwark the night following, produced so sudden an effect that before day Cade was deserted by most of his followers; who returning home, left him to shift for himself.

Perceiving that his affairs were now become desperate, Cade thought it advisable to provide for his own safety, together with that of his rich booty, which he sent by water to Rochester; and he himself in disguise fled into the woody part of Sussex.

A proclamation was issued by the government, offering 1000 marks to any person that should bring him, either dead or alive. He was discovered lurking in a garden at Hothfield in Sussex, by Alexander Eden, a Kentish gentleman, who killed him, and, having put his body into a cart, brought it to London, where he received the promised reward.

His head with those of nine of his associates, were placed on London Bridge; and some other of the ringleaders were tried and executed. Quiet was thus restored; but the dispersed populace carried home with them sentiments, which fomenting the public discontent, disposed the people to listen to the duke of York's pretensions, which now became a general topic of discussion."

Sir William Stafford of Grafton

The details in this biography come from the History of Parliament, a biographical dictionary of Members of the House of Commons.

Born by 1512, second son of Sir Humphrey Stafford of Blatherwycke and Dodford, by Margaret, dau. of Sir John Fogge of Ashford, Kent. Married first, 1533/4, Mary, daughter of Thomas Boleyn, Earl of Wiltshire and Earl of Ormond, widow of William Carey (d. 22 Jun 1538), of Aldenham, Herts., s. p.. Married second, by 1552, Dorothy, daughter of Henry Stafford, 1st Baron Stafford, and had 3 sons, Edward, John and William, and one daughter, Elizabeth. Knighted 23 Sep 1545. Esquire of the body by 1541; gentleman pensioner 1540; standard bearer, gentleman pensioner by 20 May 1550-3.

William Stafford could boast Royal descent, but as the younger son of a midland family whose fortunes had been depleted during the previous century he had little hope of advancement before his marriage to Mary Boleyn, an ex-mistress of Henry VIII.

He attended the coronation of Queen Anne Boleyn as a servitor and this may have been the occasion of his meeting with her sister whom he could have known, however, through his Kentish relatives. Their marriage displeased the King and Queen, as well as Cromwell, and Mary Boleyn told the minister that love had triumphed over reason and that although she 'might have had a greater man of birth and higher' she was content to lead 'a poor honest life' with her youthful husband.

It was perhaps the Queen's coolness towards the pair which protected them when disaster struck her and her brother Lord Rochford: in the event they were gainers, for between 1539 and 1542 Mary Stafford was to inherit in succession her father's lands, those held in jointure by Rochford's widow and those of her grandmother the Countess of Ormond.

Although the bulk of this property was to pass to the children of her first marriage, she was able to give her husband several manors in Essex, including Rochford which they later made their home. In 1541 Stafford acquired the manor of Hendon in Kent from the crown but several months later he exchanged it for more valuable property in Yorkshire and London.

After Mary's death he inherited the manor of Abinger, Surrey, which he later sold to Edward Elrington and his cousin Thomas.

In 1544 he fought in France and in 1545 in Scotland, where he was knighted by Edward Seymour, Earl of Hertford. It was doubtless as a Protestant courtier and a soldier known to Hertford (by then Protector and Duke of Somerset) that he was returned to the Parliament of 1547: the elector of Hastings had no part in the matter, for the indenture was evidently returned to the lord warden, Sir Thomas Cheney, bearing one name only, that of John Isted, and it was Cheney who added Stafford's. He was to be joined in the Commons by his stepson Henry Carey, one of the Members for Buckingham, and by his stepdaughter's husband, Sir Francis Knollys, who sat for Camelford.

Nothing is known of Stafford's role in the House, but if his second marriage had either taken place or was in contemplation he may have supported the Act for the restitution of Baron Stafford (I Edward VI, no. 18) passed during the first session, and it was either he or Henry Stafford who in the last session was licensed on 22 Feb 1552 to be absent when suffering from measles.

He was not harmed by the Protector's fall: in 1550 Somerset's rival the Earl of Warwick granted him an annuity of 100 pounds for his services to Henry VIII and entrusted him with the custody of three noble French hostages from Dover to London. In 1551 he accompanied Edward, Lord Clinton to Paris for the christening of one of Henri II's sons and on his return he took part in the New Year's tournament at court. He showed his loyalty to Northumberland by reporting a servant's allegation that the Protector had been innocent of the charges laid against him.

Whether this act assured Northumberland of his support is not known, nor whether he sat in the next Parliament summoned early in 1553 under the duke's aegis: John Isted was re-elected for Hastings but the name of his fellow-Member on this occasion has not been discovered. A brawl with Adrian Poynings in the previous Nov had reduced his standing in the Council's esteem and had led to a brief recommittal to the Fleet Prison.

Although Stafford's second marriage linked him more closely to the peerage, it brought him no wealth. In the early 1550s he disposed of much of the property given him by Mary Boleyn, and mounting debts induced him in 1552 to exchange his annuity for 900 pounds in cash.

Accompanied by his wife, children, sister, cousin and servants, he settled in Geneva in Mar 1554, being known there as Lord Rochford. He soon became embroiled in its disputes and on returning there after the uprising of 1555 he was nearly killed in an affray.

When the English congregation was set up he joined it and his son John was the first child to be baptised on 4 Jan 1556, Calvin standing as godfather.

Stafford died there on May 5, 1556, but the Privy Council was unaware of this when ten days later it ordered that 'no payment of money by exchange or otherwise' was to reach him. Calvin claimed the custody of his son John and forbade his widow to leave with him. She appealed to Stafford's younger brother and the threat to invoke French aid persuaded Calvin to yield.

She then moved to Basle, remaining there until Jan 1559, when she returned to England through aid provided by Queen Elizabeth, probably at the request of Dorothy's father, Henry Stafford, Baron Stafford, who was serving the Queen as a Courtier at the time.

The Queen recognised Lady Dorothy as a relative, the wife of her uncle Sir William Stafford whom she knew when she was a child. Elizabeth, whom she outlived, appointed her mistress of the robes; the Queen and Dorothy became close friends and Dorothy served as a trusted confidante. Dorothy served the Queen faithfully in that position for 40 years.

Dear Reader

My mother, christened Muriel; to friends and relations Aunt Tommie, or to her immediate family, Mishie, left a notebook in which she had written, in 1992, the beginnings of her auto-biography.

We had all encouraged her to write this, because our childhood was filled with the wonderful stories of her own upbringing. Alas, the notes she left only encompassed her early life. However, these few pages that I have transcribed, almost exactly as she wrote them, offer us a truly memorable glimpse of those distant and seemingly innocent days from a hundred years ago.

It has been a delight for me, immersed again in her childhood world, to relive with her those adventures, escapades and observations she has so beautifully described for us.

I have been able to include photographs gleaned from our archives to flavour her story, and I do hope you enjoy this small precious glimpse into a joyful childhood and the happy family that lived in Edwardian Derby.

Tony Stafford
February 2010

Mishie (second from right) as a small girl at her first school.

I remember .... I remember ...."

The autobiography of Muriel Elizabeth Stafford (nee Walton)

1909 -2006

I was born at the Bank House, Westminister Bank, Normanton Road, Derby – the fourth daughter of Thomas and Ethel Walton.

My parents were married in Leicester on the 30th September 1898 – Father had bought a small villa which stood in splendid isolation on Normanton Road and there is a photograph of it with a large union jack flag flying from the upstairs windows – father had a propensity for flags and later at "69" we had a flag pole in the garden.

I don't remember the Bank House, but I know Mother had a German governess for the three elder girls – Gwen, Margaret (later called Judy – when she was Auntie Judy of "Children's Hour" on Newcastle-on-Tyne's BBC programme) and Dorothea.

The tale goes that the governess, whose name now escapes me, was inordinately fond of Madeira cake, which was served in the nursery, and the two elder girls filled her tea-cup with a slice of cake, covering it with tea – pandemonium reigned – and Father had to come up from the Bank to deal with the situation.

Hysteria on the part of the Governess; alas I don't remember her, but a letter from her to my mother, found years later, contains this remark of my birth – "the poor little Muriel – nobody wanted another girl ....". I was so amazed to read this – I must have been about 16 or 17 years as never never had I felt I was the unwanted 4th daughter.

I think my parents were really remarkable – I always felt and I am sure I was as much loved as all the family, but it was four years before the longed-for son appeared.

My really first recollection must have been the day we moved from The Bank House to 69 Rose Hill Street. I don't know the exact date of our move to "69" – Father was obviously promoted Manager to the large Westminister Bank near the Station and being a countryman at heart, he had to have exercise, so he bought "69" near The Arboretum as also it had the tennis courts nearby and he could walk to the office in about 10-15 minutes, four times a day, which he did all his life. Even after we acquired a car, he never used it for going to The Bank.

Rose Hill street in 1912 was a really desirable home; very pleasant with the Arboretum leading off it and with neat and quite spacious villas opposite "69", and Dr Potter's large and rather gloomy house on the corner opposite the Arboretum gates. Going towards Normanton Road, the houses became smaller and terraced.

"69" had been the end one of three Georgian attached villas, the one in the middle being completely unchanged, but either end had been enlarged and "69" became really big with an additional four bedrooms and nursery and with an attic was in all five stories, with a total of seven bedrooms and father's dressing room, but only one bathroom and separate lavatory, and with a further lavatory downstairs out of the back kitchen for the maid!

The sitting room, drawing room, dining room and big lounge had French windows on to the garden and my first recollection when we moved was in the evening tea-time of that day. There was quite a step up to the French window and I remember having a glass of milk and plate of biscuits on the step which seemed like a long table as I sat on the floor, being about three years old and then the baby of the family.

It must have been before we moved to "69" that Father went on his cycling trip to Cumberland. He and Mother had been away for the night, almost unheard of, and for some reason he had gone into a barbers to have a haircut and a shave; quite a common thing to do in those days; in fact some hotels had their own barbers shop. This was in the days of "cut-throat razors", which Father always used and I can hear him now in his dressing room 'stropping' away – the strop was pliable, almost like leather, about 3 inches wide and 12 to 18 inches long. It was attached to the wall and the blade of the razor was stropped as you would a carving knife on a steel. Anyway, he caught erisipilis[26], which is highly contagious; you come out with a rash on your face and so can't shave.

Of course he couldn't appear in the Bank, so he had three weeks leave, cycling around the Lake District. Taking the train to Carlisle, he called and stayed with his second cousin, James Atkinson, who farmed at Brackenthwaite with his brother, John, and sister, Elizabeth, who looked after them.

It could have been around the time I was born, as he went alone, Mother being 'enceinte'[27] (lovely expression!) and Elizabeth was subsequently my Godmother. She left me a beautifully chased gold pocket watch, which I remember Mother showing it to me when I was

---

[26] *Contagious infection of the skin and underlying tissue caused by group A B-haemolytic streptococcus bacteria. Erysipelas causes affected areas of skin to turn bright red and become slightly swollen. The swollen blotches have a distinct border and slowly expand into the surrounding skin. The lesions are most commonly seen on the face, scalp, hands, and legs. They feel hot to the touch and the patient is feverish. Centuries ago erysipelas epidemics caused severe and often fatal infections.*

[27] *une femme enceinte - expectant mother*

about seven, but have never seen it since!! However, the silk crinoline frocks came from Brackenthwaite.

I make this digression because James must have died before we moved to "69", because most of the big furniture came from Brackenthwaite. There was a wonderful wooden milking churn which stood in the hall in which we kept our hockey and lacrosse sticks; the tennis rackets, balls and garden rugs were kept in the old oak settle.

However, Father must have made a great impression with the three Atkinson's, both brothers being bachelors and Elizabeth a spinster. James, the elder, did a lot in the parish of Cumrew, and James[28] left Brackenthwaite to father, which annoyed his elder brother, Edmund (Edmund Walton's grandfather).

When I was four, I was driven to Melton Mowbray to stay with Aunt Dora. Her husband, Uncle Ned, was manager of the Westminister Bank there. They lived in the Bank House, a lovely old house, but with no garden, but Uncle had a garden some way away by the river, where he also had a boat, and used to row us occasionally.

I can remember the drive to Melton Mowbray. It was an open car, a Bouton de Dijon, and Mr and Mrs Archbutt took me; I think Father must have been with us too; but I remember Mrs Archbutt donning a dust coat and tying her hat on with a large beige scarf.

I think the Archbutts had been out in the Far East, certainly their son, Charlie, whom we all loved dearly, was out there, and I rather think he was with the East India Company. His parents lived in little double fronted house in Madley Street, and the garden at the back opened onto the tennis courts, as did ours.

I don't remember anything of that visit to Melton, Peter and I went again later, but the house was fascinating. Downstairs was a square hall opening on the right to the Bank itself, and on the left a very large, dark and forbidding dining room, which I always associate with my cousin Barbara having fights with her mother over food; spinach and cabbage; both of which were overcooked and ghastly and we had to eat it.

The kitchens were light and large down a passage and a very wide and important staircase led through a wonderful bead curtain to a square landing and a very large sitting room with two or three windows looking on to the street. Fascinating – always something to watch. Other bedrooms and then down a long passage with more bedrooms, bathroom and study and then up backstairs to a wonderful nursery and even more bedrooms.

---

[28] *James died on 27th April 1907, aged 82. Elizabeth died 30th October 1909, aged about 77*

Aunt Dora had two children, Barbara and Myles. Barbara was about Judy's age, a dark, sultry girl, who was at art school in Nottingham (I think) and very gifted. It was in the early twenties when the late Duke of Windsor, then Prince of Wales, was hunting a lot and various houses were taken a 'hunting boxes', a gay life was led, and they were known as 'the Prince of Wales Set'. I believe Barbara got a bit mixed up with them and fearful family rows ensued and eventually she took some job in London. The next thing I knew (Mother probably knew a lot more, but remember I was only about twelve at the time and nothing of that nature was ever discussed) was that she married a man called Pickup (appropriate I felt at the time) and I never saw her again.

Myles, her brother, trained as a dentist – another cause for a furore. I think he had just got qualified and taken into partnership in Grantham, when after hectic telephone calls from Aunt Dora to Mother; I came across Mother sorting out old baby clothes etc and was told Myles was going to get married!! However no baby appeared – at least not for two or three years. I have only vague recollections of him and his blonde wife, whom I always thought Aunt Dora regarded as 'fast' - probably quite unkindly.

Well – I came back from Melton Mowbray to find a large pram under the veranda – of course brother Peter lying there. He was called Thomas Atkinson, after Father and we girls used to chant Big Tom, little Tom, which made Father mad!!

Peter and I were good friends, although four years divided us. Thea, although only 2½ years older, was too grown-up and I hardly recall playing with her; but, of course, we were great friends in adulthood.

Two incidents remain clear. One was the taking of the Photograph of us three younger ones. I was deputised to 'watch' Peter, ready, dressed and waiting for the taxi to take us to the Photographers. I was dressed in the white embroidery anglaise dress, knickers and petticoat to match and I can still recall the starch scratching my legs!!

I was allowed, as a great favour, to hold .... a big doll with the china face; the first and last time. Peter was crawling around the dining room floor when someone came into the room and at me - "Peter is in the coal bucket". Imagine – I dropped the doll – the head broke – pandemonium. Peter was hastily washed and changed as the taxi was waiting. The shoe bag with our bronze dancing and white socks (we couldn't walk outside in those); black socks and lace-up shoes was Thea's responsibility as she was nearly seven years old. Alas, when we got to the photographers, Thea's white silk socks were not in the bag, so she is wearing her black ones – hence the scowl!!

About the same time, I used to play 'horses' riding on the arms of the big chairs in the lounge, and Peter wanted to join in. So I managed to get on the other arm and away we went, jogging for dear life. Of course, Peter fell off and Mother in coat, hat and veil rushed him round to the Doctors as there was no car in those days and no time to call a taxi, which had to be ordered the day before. He had a 'green stick' fracture of his arm, which was set very badly, and he always had a terrific bump on his elbow. I remember him lying later in his cot and Mother feeding him with mashed bananas and cream, which I was not allowed. That was my punishment; oh dear, I did seem to lead Peter into trouble but he was quite a lot younger and I didn't realise he couldn't always manage to keep up with me.

I had just learnt to slide down the banisters. It was a very wide solid mahogany banister rail and really long. One Sunday afternoon, i was very bored and started sliding down the banisters. Father and Mother were having a nap in the lounge. Peter joined me, and, of course, fell slap into the china bowl – oh dear – bedlam and bed!!

Our nursery was at the top of the house – up four flights of stairs (the attics were one higher), with a wonderful view over the roof tops right over to Normanton. It was a big room. Imagine maids lighting fires and carrying coals up there!! Mother had a sewing woman, a Miss Greatorex, who cycled about 7 to 10 miles in from the country once a month for three or four days to help with the mending and making frocks for us.

We all loved her dearly and were horrified when she got married. I must have been 13 or 14, as she made all our school frocks when I joined Thea at Harrogate at school. She was the only person Thea would let pull her teeth out when they became loose. We never told father if we had a loose tooth as he thought he was the 'great puller-out of tooth's', and if he caught you, a piece of sewing cotton was tied around the offending tooth, the other end to an open door handle, then slam the door and hey presto, the deed was done, with a slightly bloody mouth and the tooth on the end of the cotton to be placed under the pillow for a three penny bit the next morning.

We certainly never had another governess after Peter was born, as the three elder girls all went to the Derby High school where father was the Hon. Secretary. He held that post until he died, and when a new building and assembly room was built it was dedicated to him and Archbishop FitzHerbert. In fact it was said that "Mr Walton was the Derby High School".

But we must have had a nursery maid. I remember Rose used to take us for walks in the holidays; all five of us and always up to Normanton where the barracks were, now alas demolished; but it was lovely to see the sentries on duty. I think her 'admirer' was a soldier. It was country lanes up there. Down the lane from the barracks was a slaughter house – Gwen used to hold us by the door and try and make us peer in – horrid!

In the same way, if we went past the Barracks, we came to Normanton station, and when the trains started again, all the smoke came over the bridge; really clouds upon clouds of smoke, so acid, and Gwen used to catch us and make us stand in it - it hurt your eyes. But it was all country lanes with hedgerows of hawthorn, which in the spring we called 'head and cheese' and used to chew.

In the summer, we had a church fete in somebody's garden off the Burton road, so Mother, Peter and I walked there; at least Peter on his tricycle sharing rides with me. Father was at the Fete, but I think he went by taxi as few people had cars. We really did walk miles. No, I think Father did walk; he was a great walker, but not with the younger children. Anyway, it was a house with quite a nice garden, but a lovely steep grassy bank; and Peter spent the whole of the afternoon sliding down this. When Mother came to collect him, he had worn two holes in his cotton trousers!! You can imagine green and holely. Mother couldn't possibly have him walking home like that, so he rode all the way home and I had to walk!!

Mother had a friend, Mrs Toft, who lived fairly near, with three children, Betty, Pauline and Tom, who were friends of the three older ones, and we all used to go out on picnics. Really it was an outing. We firstly had the maids make up the picnic basket, and then we had to walk to the station, take a train out to Cox Bench[29]; get out, stop at the village shop for lemonade, a glass bottle with a glass marble at the top which you pushed down, and could then drink the lemonade – lovely!

We would then walk to the favourite place to picnic. I must have been about 8 or 9, as Peter at 4 or 5 had to walk a good way, though the big girls used to join hands and make a chair to give him a lift. Sometimes, one of our favourite places was a hill with trees on the far side and beautifully grassy on our ascent with lots of rabbit holes, which delighted the dogs; a black spaniel called Luck, ruined for shooting said Father, because he lived in the house and not in Castle Carrock with Headington, the keeper. A terrier, whether it was Violet or Rinnons, I can't remember.

The hill was known as Bunker's Hill, so named after the Boer War. I clearly remember the fear of looking down the wooded side as I feared seeing dead soldiers with the spiked helmets of German soldiers, which I

---

[29] *Coxbench is a tiny settlement situated off the Alfreton Road, just past Little Easton when travelling from Derby.. It once had its own railway station, the buildings of which are still standing and are a private residence*

must have seen in the Illustrated London News, a magazine we had weekly. I never remember reading a daily paper until I was in my teens.

However, after peering and re-assurance from Peter, in whom I confided, I ventured on the tree side of the hill, where all was well; and where, on one occasion, I found a hedgehog, which I carried home in my beret and which was promptly banished by Father to the conservatory.

The conservatory was really Edwardian. It was outside the lounge, which had two very large French windows – one to the garden and the other to the conservatory. There was a little pool in the middle and was built around with rocks, from which greenery grew – ferns etc. with two sides growing right up to the windows. Mother had a geranium which was enormous and her pride and joy. We had sort of miniature palms and at one time – tree frogs, which were bright green and changed their colour according to the leaves they were on.

The conservatory is where one of my hedgehogs expired (I seemed to collect hedgehogs on my walks). I was sitting in the lounge sewing on name tapes before going back to school. I must have left the door ajar leading to the conservatory and pip, the terrier, got in. I heard nothing until he emerged with a red muzzle. He had managed to uncurl poor old Tiggywinkle and that was the end of him!!

When I was about 4 years old, I was allowed on sunny summer mornings to accompany the elder girls, as far as the Arboretum, to school. I can remember feeling very grown up; waving them good-bye and trotting home by myself. This was the Madeley Street entrance; a little further than the big entrance in Rose Hill Street. It was in Madeley Street that I always had to stroke a chow-chow dog that wandered up and down. One day, it jumped up and bit the back of my neck, and that was what made me so terrified of dog fights.

I particularly remember the purchasing of our summer hats. Mother used to take us by train down to St James Street in the centre of Derby, where there was a hat shop. The hats were made for us - velours in the winter and panamas in the summer, with a blue or pink ribbon and then daisies and forget-me-nots fastened under the ribbon by their stalks so the flower heads lay along the brim and danced up and down when you ran and skipped. I loved wearing that hat.

Mother never dreamt of going out without a hat or gloves, and nearly always a veil. She was so pretty. When i was quite little I used to wear gaiters. They were made of leather and lined with stockinet and had buttons all the way up and had to be done up with a button hook.

Father was blessed with the amazing capacity of being able to communicate with all stratas of society and in my young days these were indeed well defined. Amongst his many customers (is that the correct word?) was an old couple, Mr and Mrs Martin. He had been a butler and she, a cook, on some big estate. They had remained in service until their retirement, had no family, and had bought quite a large corner villa, about 20 minutes walk from "69". We had to visit them at least twice a year; and once a year had tea, when we were given tinned salmon; something we never had at home. I loved it because the bones were all soft and you could eat them.

They, or rather Mrs Martin, adored Peter and one winter when he was about three years old, she gave him, to Mother's horror, a white fur muffler and tippet; that is a little flat fur collar with a sort of jabot[30] in front. Of course, Peter adored it and insisted on wearing it, much to Mother's chagrin; and, of course, always on the visits. Mother did manage to spirit it away betimes. Later on we used to tricycle up there, sharing the trike, of course. They had a wonderfully neat little garden, really; with 'cockle shells' where we sat primly on a bench.

As they got older, we didn't really want to go; the house had a peculiar odour, never a window opened. Fortunately, Mrs Martin could no longer manage the teas. There were always a few tears and lots of kissing on our leave-taking, and packets of biscuits given to us, which were always stale! I am so glad Mother made us go, as obviously it gave them great delight. I remember seeing one of them in bed; Mr Martin, I think, and he died soon after. They had, during the years, bought quite a lot of terrace houses by the Railway Carriage and Wagon Works. These they left to Father in their will and I have a feeling they were eventually intended for Peter, but alas he died in India and they came to us girls.

Father had a sister, Annie, who lived with her husband at Kegworth - Springwell House. They had two children, Kathleen, my dearest cousin – so much older than me, but always so kind to me, and Hubert.Springwell House was delightful with the front on the Kegworth to Leicester road and a doctor's family living next door. I can't remember the name, but do remember one of the sons, whom I went out with occasionally.

Aunt Annie had a lovely garden with quite a large lawn and numerous outbuildings. Uncle kept goats for a time. The garden descended into terraces with eventually the drive going down to the Derby to Loughborough Road. If this part has not been built on, I am sure this entrance must be blocked as the road must now be extremely busy.

---

[30] *An ornamental cascade of ruffles or frills down the front of a shirt, blouse, or dress*

Aunt Annie was extremely deaf; the result of having scarlet fever as a child. But she had a beautiful, serene face and always wore a black velvet band around her neck and very often with some jewel threaded on to it. Hubert, the son, was very clever, electrically. I remember, fairly young, seeing Aunt opening cupboards, with a light going on immediately, commonplace now, but magical then.

Hubert later became the celebrated electrical firm of Partridge and Wilson in Leicester. They built the first electric car. During Hubert's childhood, they had a boat and boathouse on the River Soar – rowing, of course. I well remember his 21st birthday when I was about 8 or 9. It was to be a river picnic and very simple by today's standard. Anyway, I suppose we all must have been invited and although I remember so little about it, barring the fact that Thea and I were told to wear our navy skirts and jumpers. Imagine our chagrin when a girl, certainly a few years older than Thea, appeared in white, with a full length knitted cloak – for a water picnic!! I don't remember if we had a flotilla of boats, but certainly they were all rowing boats.

Stella, the vision in white, and who simpered all day (we thought she was ghastly) eventually married Hubert and called herself, Estelle. They had three children; Elizabeth, who was my older bridesmaid, was a very good child rider, and rode at the Dublin Horse Show, and eventually married a young man whose father made a fortune out of soap powders. She was a very unhappy woman, and died young.

Catherine, the second girl, married a Baronet's younger son, and they had some tragedy in the family. Bill, the only son, lived with his mother after his parents separated. Hubert died years before Kathleen and I have completely lost touch with them. Kathleen was a lovely girl and was a V.A.D. during the 14-18 war. (that is – a nurse). She married her second cousin, Hamilton Hartridge, against much opposition of both parents.

Father always said that Sophie Hartridge, Hamilton's mother, was one of the kindest women. When I was training at St Thomas's, I found her rather formidable. They had a flat in St James and a small country estate in Surrey, but i forget the name. I only saw her a few times, small and very erect, being chauffeur driven around London in a Rolls-Royce; great kudos, but me hardly remember her husband. They had three children; Hamilton, his brother – was it Keith, and sister, who never married, was very plain, but remembered by me as she had been presented at court!!

Keith lived with a friend in Hampstead and used to come to various occasions at Hamilton and Kathleen's family. I never gave it a thought that it was odd for two men to live together; so much better than this present flaunting of 'gay' men.

Hamilton was a brilliant man. He had been at Harrow and was a life Governor of the school. When I was in London, they lived in ..sett? Terrace, very close to Hyde Park. Amongst other things, he was a member of the Geographical Society, so I could go to the London Zoo on Sundays!!! They had four children, Anne, Gerald, Felicity (my bridesmaid) and Jennifer. I spent quite a lot of Sundays with them and they were so kind to me. I remember going for walks with them and their nanny in Hyde Park. Jennifer being a 'new' baby, in the pram, and we used to go to the Round pond and Peter Pan's statue.

Hamilton was devoted to his children and on Sunday evenings when the maids were out, we used to go down into the kitchen, a lovely big airy one in the basement (I expect now converted into a flat or flatso and make marzipan mice!! I was at Jenny's christening, but soon after I finished my training, they moved to Northwood and a lovely house and garden. But I'm getting beyond myself.

I went to the Kindergarten of the High School when I was five years. It was in Hartington Street, where the main school was. We were allowed to take a toy, but it had to be kept on a wire rack outside the school room. I don't remember much about school then but I do remember the dancing classes. Miss Stevens and Miss Dark ran the Kindergarten, but Miss Stevens took the dancing class, which was wonderful.

Miss Stevens wore a dress that had an accordion pleated skirt, which spread like a fan when she raised her hands above her head. I thought it quite wonderful. We all arrived with our shoe-bags containing white silk socks and our bronze dancing shoes. The best shoes had little rosettes on the front. I loved every minute of the class, my hair bobbing on my shoulders and imagined myself a true ballerina.

It wasn't till years later that Mother, who sat with the other mums said – "You really dance quite nicely now, but, oh dear, those early classes; you were like a marionette, your feet didn't belong to your legs – they shot out at all angles"!!! At least she didn't say it until I had got some co-ordination and I could laugh about it.

I went to the High School until I was about 12 or 13, when I joined Thea at Elmwood School in Harrogate. It wasn't easy as Aunt Eva, Mother's youngest sister, was joint headmistress with her great friend, Mrs Hogben. Aunt Eva was the youngest of the four girls. Grandfather Charters had a boot and shoe factory in Leicester with a cousin as co-director. Grandfather and grandmother (whom, alas, I never knew) had nine children – Beatrice, Ethel (Mother), Frank, Dorothea (Dora), Ernest (?), Phillip, Maurice, Geoffrey and Eva.

Beatrice, who was very musical, was sent to Germany for two years to study music and subsequently got her L.R.A.M. Mother was also sent to a finishing school at Lausanne. Frank went into a bank. I think the other boys were still at the Wiggestone School in Leicester. Maurice was playing cricket in the late summer when he was hit on the head by, I think, a cricket ball – anyway he subsequently died, which upset the entire family; Grandfather, tremendously. In the same winter he took a heavy cold. He had a great friend who lived at Badgreve Hall (now a museum, I remember going there as a child), the other side of Leicester, who sent a note asking him to urgently go and see him. He had dismissed his coachman for the night and so he walked to see him. On his return, it was raining and he got extremely wet and got pneumonia which led to his untimely death.

Poor Grandmamma was left with eight children to set on their careers.

MISHIE
20th March 1909 – 7th March 2006

passing through ... my Life

My Life

an autobiography

Introduction

I suppose most of us, at one point in our lives, want to record something of what has happened in those years gone past, and to pass that story on to our children and grandchildren. Of course, whether they really want to read the ramblings of an egotistical ancestor is another matter!

I have tried in this small book to bring interest and humour to the reader; and not, hopefully, to indulge in too much whimsy and glorification.

I'm not sure whether there is much glory there anyway, but I hope my life will be seen as being well lived; and that, for all my errors and omissions, one can say that at the least .... I had a go.

A War baby

At least my father had some leave during the war. Wouldn't it have been awful if he had been captured during the Battle for Norway in 1941, or been kept in Iceland for the duration. I might then have been a post war baby, and missed all the excitement and opportunity that I've had in my life!

But, thankfully, in September 1942, he managed to get a week or so at home in North Warwickshire; at Witherley Lodge, a large Georgian house built on the old Roman Watling Street as it leads westward through Atherstone. And so it was there, in the front bedroom, that I was born on Sunday morning, 27th June 1943.

My two elder sisters, Jennifer and Angela, must have been thrilled to have a baby brother; although it would be apparent, particularly after my younger sister, Virginia, was born eighteen months later; that as the only boy, I was going to be spoilt rotten!

Like so many others, my parents were having to battle with all the emotions, privations and horror of a World war. At that point in 1943, the tide was beginning to turn in our favour. They had endured the bombings of Coventry and Leicester in 1940/1, and although the Midlands area was considerably safer than London and the south, everybody was affected by the very strict rationing restrictions and the absence of most of the men fighting a long war.

My father, Ernest, had been in the Territorial Army since the mid thirties. In fact, it was because he had joined the Sherwood Foresters, that he had met up with Peter Walton, and then with Peter's sister, Muriel. They had married on the 5th May 1934 and set up home at Witherley. Dad had been working at the family hat-making business since leaving boarding school, whilst Muriel, or Tommy[31] as all her friends called her, had studied as a physiotherapist at St Thomas's Hospital in London, and latterly at the Chailey Heritage[32] special school

---

[31] *As a young girl, she had been very close to her younger brother, Peter, and was regarded as a "tomboy" – hence Tommie.*

[32] *Chailey Heritage Hospital was founded in 1903 by Grace Kimmins and Alice Rennie. It is world-famous for its ground-breaking approach to orthopaedics. Originally it offered hospital treatment, education and training in craftwork to children with severe physical disabilities. Much of the philosophy of care derived from Grace Kimmins' husband, Dr C W Kimmins, who was an educational psychologist for the London County Council. Chailey Heritage was initially a private institution and relied heavily on donations for its survival. Grace Kimmins tirelessly and inventively raised funds for the hospital. She was well-connected and used her contacts to secure the patronage and support of royalty, the aristocracy, affluent businessmen and the press.*

for children with complex physical disabilities, near Lewes in East Sussex.

In 1942, my father had been posted to Reykjavik, Iceland as a staff officer. From there he returned to a course at the Camberley Staff College, before joining the Allied Headquarters Staff engaged in planning the Normandy landings. With the ending of the war in 1945, he was posted to Hanover as the Deputy Military Governor.

The little soldier

Of the few memories I have of being a very little boy, two remain astonishingly clear. The first was the thrill of having a dunk in a large galvanised tub in the walled garden by the side of the house during the hot summer of 1947. The other was standing by the road outside the front of the house with a toy rifle and saluting the immense convoys of American soldiers who were being driven back to Liverpool docks on their way home. To their credit, I got many salutes in return, and possibly that might have been the catalyst for my desire to join the Services in later years.

With Daddy back home, things became more normal, although rationing was still in force and there were no luxuries or expensive presents to be bought. However, we had what I remember as an idyllic childhood. Mummy, of course, did not work, and had the huge benefit of a live-in maid and a gardener. Bread arrived daily by bicycle, as did milk; and meat and groceries were delivered when required. We even had a weekly arrival of fish direct from Grimsby, which always came in a flat woven grass bag.

Dolly Tilson was both our maid and my solace when times got tough, if I didn't get my way; or, particularly at night, when the creaking's of an old house became too much for my imagination! It was then that I crept from the bedroom I shared with Ginger, along a small passage and climbed up the curly stairs to Dolly's bedroom on the floor above. There was no heating up there next to the attics, and I used to scramble quickly into the cosy warmth of her single iron bed. She would never refuse me. Dolly was a lovely, simple person. At that time she would have been about forty years old; a homely open face and a rather shapeless body, but a heart of gold, and a manner of kissing that sounded rather like a machine gun being fired. Real smackers!

Since their marriage in 1934, my parents had had a number of servants, although none had stayed for very long. Dolly had been "in service" with us since I was four and was to stay until, amazingly, she married Bill, a huntsman at the local kennels, in 1958.

Although I was a fit and healthy child in most respects, I did manage to contract osteomylitis when I was seven and then had another attack in the other leg a year later. This infection attacks the growing end of the bone and can cause it to stop developing with dire results. It was particularly painful, I remember, and as treatment was in hospital, I seemed to spend a lot of time at the Manor[33] in Nuneaton. Luckily, penicillin had just become available on the new National Health Service, and three injections a day eventually sorted me out with no residual limp. In 1951, when I was just eight, Dolly was left in charge when Mum and Dad went on a short holiday to Ireland. Playing a game of hide and seek with my younger sister, Ginger; I hid beside the Aga cooker, pulled a tea towel over me and with it the contents of a saucepan of boiling stock – right over my head! Dolly panicked and wrapping me in a blanket, rushed to a small cottage next door to find out what to do. Luckily for me they rang the doctor immediately and he, an ambulance – so what was a certainly a very nasty accident luckily did not cause my early demise!

Time for school

My first school was in Mancetter, just across the fields in front of the house. It was part of another old Georgian house with a large garden sweeping down to the River Anker. I was about five then and truthfully remember very little about my lessons or the teacher. I do recall with pleasure the walk over the fields to a little narrow gantry bridge that took us over the river past the Mill. There was a sty next door occupied by three or four large pink pigs, and I think my fascination with these animals must have started from this point; although I can still recall the awful squeals when our own pig at Witherley was slaughtered.

In 1950, my proper schooling started at Grendon Lodge, the home of my very best friend and cousin, Clive Vero. State education was still a hit and miss affair just after the war, and a group of concerned parents had got together to start a small day school in two classrooms in the old servants quarters of this large and commodious Victorian house. Mrs Acton and Mrs Forrest were our mistresses, and for three years I enjoyed the most perfect time there. When we were a little older, we were allowed to catch the Midland Red bus back from the town. The fare was one penny!

It was in those days the "done" thing in the middle and upper classes, for one's children to go away to boarding school. First to a Preparatory School for perhaps five or six years, and then on to the

---

[33] *By coincidence, I became Vice Chairman of it's successor, The George Eliot, in 1994*

great Public Schools until the age of 18 or 19, finishing probably at University.

By this time, Jenny and Angie had already started boarding, both of them going to Stamford High School. Just before my ninth birthday, it was my turn. I remember being taken to various schools for my parents to judge its' worthiness and for me, presumably, to be looked over by the headmasters as to my suitability. Eventually, it was decided that St Hugh's School, near Faringdon in Oxfordshire was going to be the place for me. I had no choice! And so on the 8th of January 1953, I was left rather inconsolably, at Carswell Manor, under the tutelage of the rather forbidding figure of the elderly Headmaster, Raymond Tootell MA, and Miss Allard, the Matron.

Forts and Floppies

As my parents drove away in the Bentley, I realised I was on my own for the first time in my life. The elder boys of 12 or 13 seemed enormous. The house was austere and huge, a labyrinth of rooms from floor to floor, full of strange faces, voices and bodies rushing hither and thither. Presumably I did get sorted out, and my only memory of that day was climbing into a narrow iron-framed bed in a dormitory of 12, between cold hard starched sheets and feeling very, very lonely!

After three weeks or so, I had become one of the gang. We were in the White Dorm, on the ground floor. Above us was the Blue Dorm. Apparently, the current fad was after "lights out", to gather at the big bay window and pass comics and tuck in a basket hauled up to the boys above. It seemed we must have made too much noise that particular night, for suddenly the Headmaster was there, catching us all red-handed..... we each got three whacks on the bottom with his slipper ... I don't think I'd ever been punished like that before - and home seemed a long way away from my cold hard bed at Carswell Manor. It was my introduction to corporal punishment. Unfortunately, I did not learn too much from that experience and beatings became a feature of my school life, although, thankfully, fairly infrequently!

Carswell was a large Jacobean Manor house set in about 12 acres of parkland some 5 miles from Faringdon in Oxfordshire. The front of the house was lawned to a "Ha-Ha"[34], and beyond that lay eight acres of playing fields surrounded on the three sides by a 200 yard belt of woodland. The woods to the left were our playground. Here we became the stuff of our imaginations. Robin Hoods, King Arthurs, Biggles or any or all of our heroes. And here we were "allowed" to build forts, to have

---

[34] *A concealed stone fronted sloping ditch, designed to keep cattle away from the house, without spoiling the view with fences or hedges.*

mock battles with other gangs, to have huge adventures, and simply to have the best time ever.

I can still remember vividly the weekly bath, sitting in those funny little invalid baths, the ones with the raised seat part; with Miss Allard, the Matron, scrubbing us very vigorously. She was a little dumpling of a woman, who could be rather gruff with certainly no time for shirkers, but actually with a heart of gold. I found that out one summer Sunday, when I was convinced my parents were going to take me out. Whilst the school walked over the fields to Buckland Church, I waited and waited, but to no avail. No parents arrived, and one very miserable small boy was cheered up by a very sympathetic Matron and a very large sugar sandwich.

Of course, this was 1953, and food and luxury items were still very scarce. Amongst the fairly uninspiring food, my one culinary joy each week was sausage day. A box of chipolata sausages would arrive from some secret source, and I used to hang around by the kitchen to make sure it had come. Sausages are still my passion today!!!

The following year, Mr Tootell became very ill and his deputy, Tom Young, took over. He was so different; probably in his late thirties, a very modern and enlightened master. He became my personal hero and a man who brought so much light into our lives. He seemed to have so much enthusiasm for everything and again individually for each one of us. Without any doubt, he stood head and shoulders above any teacher I have ever known; and must have laid the secure foundations for the St Hugh's School of today.

Mr Young had lots of great schemes to add diversity to our boarding school lives. One of these was for boys to have a garden plot to grow vegetables or flowers. We all were terribly enthused by this project at first, but gardening for ten year olds gets a little boring after a while. So some wag decided to start tunnelling. It was very sandy, loamy soil - and remarkably easy to dig away in. Of course, we were all avid readers of war books, and the idea of emulating "The Great Escape" or other adventures was not far from our minds. Great efforts were made to disguise the entrances, and one fellow even fashioned out an underground room complete with an earth armchair!!! Luckily no-one was entombed and, as far as I can remember, we were never discovered ... such nice little boys.

I remember some of the Masters. Mr Dewey was a tall, amenable and very kindly man (in later life I always considered him to be the original Mr Chips). Mr Sempill, who taught Latin, was a very precise and quiet man - but there were never any disturbances in his classes! Mr Cooper, a large, florid faced gentleman, taught Geography and French. He was the antithesis of Mr Sempill and had an unerring aim with the hard wooden chalk eraser.

Under the tutelage of Tom Young, my natural shyness and inhibitions seemed to vanish, and I blossomed into a reasonably bright and sporty twelve year old. I was never a scholar or a brilliant athlete, but I coped pretty well, even becoming a prefect and Rugby captain in my last term. My biggest problem, however, was Latin!! To go to Public School, one had to pass the dreaded "Common Entrance" examination. I was reasonably confident to all the required subjects, except for Latin, in those days an absolute essential, and a language that left me utterly cold!! So twice a week in the summer holidays of 1956, I had to cycle up to Atherstone and enter the walled convent, there to be given extra tuition by the priest, Father Rainer. It was an odd experience, but despite the trials of enduring the strange silence and medicinal smells of a closed order of nuns, my marks in the Latin exam paper were excellent. So in January 1957, I entered the hallowed halls of Oundle School.

From Fagging ....

My father had picked Oundle because it had a reputation as a very good engineering school. I'm sure that if he had been able to choose his working career, he would have been in some technically related job, rather than being a Director in a Headwear company. In me, I think, he saw a substitute for his own disappointments, and I therefore had a lot of responsibility resting on my shoulders. Unfortunately, as is often the case between father and son, our relationship was not an open and confiding one. I did what I was told to do – but I was terrified of what might befall me at my big school.

In the middle fifties, before television became so dominant, reading was very popular, and I absolutely devoured books. My tastes were not, I'm afraid, particularly cultured; I had an obsession for war books and tales of the sea, and I had recently read the classic "Tom Browns Schooldays".[35] If you read this great book, you will come across the awful scene when the bully Flashman and his henchmen roast Tom in front of a blazing fire. Despite the fact that this novel had been written one hundred years earlier, I was convinced such barbarity still existed in 1957. Well, possibly a little of the old regime lingered on, but, fortunately, I remained untoasted.

To start with, I was entered into the junior house, the Berrystead, where Doctor and Mrs Tagg looked after the thirty youngest boys in a school of 750 who were resident in eleven other houses. After the intimacy of St Hugh's, this was a very different prospect. Although

---

[35] A story of a young boy's trials and tribulations at Rugby School in the middle nineteenth century.

Oundle was a market town, it was totally dominated by the school, which had been founded in 1543 and had been supported since then by the Grocer's Livery Company. The houses were scattered throughout the town, and school life centered on the Cloisters in the middle, close to Great Hall; and a little farther away, the Chapel, and the Science Buildings and Engineering Workshops. Surrounding this were the playing fields; rugby in the winter and cricket during the summer. An open air unheated swimming pool provided a degree of fun in the hotter months.

After two terms of the utterly uninspiring housemastership of the insipid Dr Tagg, I moved on to my senior house, Grafton. This was one of the four field houses, and here Mr Huse presided, assisted by his matron. Today, if you are fortunate to have very wealthy parents and go to a Boarding School, it is most likely that a young married couple will have charge of your health and welfare – to provide warmth and hopefully understanding of the problems of teenage life. In my day, unfortunately, enlightment of that kind was some way off; so I was placed in a rather austere house supervised by a fifty year old bachelor and a slightly younger, frumpy and, I'm sure, rather frustrated spinster.

George Huse meant well, but he was an ethereal and introspective person, and rather left the internal discipline and organisation of the house to the Prefects; and so the old customs of initiation and fagging were still in practice. Within a fortnight of joining the school, one was expected to memorise the "Blue Book", a termly publication detailing all the Masters, Forms, Houses and pupils. This was quite a feat and, naturally, a test which was near impossible for a twelve year old to pass. The punishment at that time was three circuits of the junior common room – simple enough you might say, except this was done around the top of the lockers and included a jump across the doorway!!

Fagging was another throwback to the good old days! Each of the five house prefects was allocated two fags. Their duty was to respond immediately, at the run, to the call of "Fag", and attend on whichever prefect called. One might be required to post a letter, shine shoes, prepare some toast; or whatever, within certain limits, took the senior's fancy. It was, of course, eminently suitable for abuse; but apart from having to rush about a bit like frightened rabbits, I don't think we came to much harm. The other more insidious area was the repressed sexuality of 70 rapidly maturing adolescents! I was, I think, quite a pretty boy, and I do remember a few instances of certain elder boys trying to entice me into an illicit situation; but, dear readers, you will be pleased to know I retained my innocence for those heterosexual delights that were to follow, slightly later on!!

.... to fags

Whilst Oundle was, without doubt, a great school, I somehow managed to mislay both my academic and games prowess; and never seemed to rise above the middle of the road, average, and regretfully, rather uninspired, mediocre. True, I did row in the fours for my house; and I did reasonably well in my workshop classes – but the advantages of a public school education passed me by.

Once I was seventeen, all I wanted to do was put school, regulation and its sexless society behind me ... and enter the real world!! So at the end of the summer term in 1960, with the cautionary lecture of the headmaster, Mr Knight, ringing in our ears (... we would never get on in life and succeed if we indulged in self-abuse!!), it was a last march down to Oundle station, crammed into the train, and light up our carefully hoarded fags; and with a casual wave to the Masters, we set off into LIFE.

My Destiny?

My early departure from education was mostly due to an absolute belief that my career in life would be as a Hatmaker, working in the family business. It seemed such a natural avenue to take. It would involve a modicum of work, a rather privileged position, and, of course, a fairly good salary after a short apprenticeship. However, it became obvious fairly early on that I had not thought this situation out very well!

Although my father had been a firm supporter of this endeavour (Mum had always thought university would have been a far better choice, and how right she was!); his ideas of how I would learn my trade were quite different from my aspirations. To start with, I was to work full factory hours. That meant an early morning cycle ride into Atherstone, and not sitting beside the boss in his Bentley arriving 2 hours later. At that time, the working week was 60 hours, and my wages were £6.00!! Dad had also decried that I should start with the finished product, the hat, and then work my way backwards through the thirty odd processes of manufacture to the point where the wool came through the door. It sounded quite a good idea, except that, once started, I seemed to be forgotten in the packing room, and apart from a stint in the dyeshop, never did get to see all the other operations. Possibly just as well. In the bowels of the felt-making department was the hardening shop. This area seemed to be populated by enormous sweaty women with huge breasts, who worked in a fog of steam and noise, operating weird rattling presses turning wool forms into felt. I was told that it was the tradition that new male apprentices were ambushed by these amazons and that their delicate areas were smothered in black grease!! In consequence of this spoof, I kept as far away as possible.

After eighteen months of a rather mundane and boring existence, I decided that "The Factory" was not, after all, the shangri-la of my dreams. To my father's absolute chagrin, I left the firm of Wilson & Stafford Limited, and found work as a barman at The Three Tuns Hotel in Long Street in Atherstone. In my father's eyes to work in a pub was horror enough, but to work in a local pub was truly awful – poor Dad! After six months behind the bar, I met the owner of a local garage, and before long I was trying to sell Vauxhall Vivas to all and sundry. I don't think that marketing was my greatest skill, although I do remember a few commission cheques arriving after I had left.

In the summer of 1963, with a few months to fill up, I applied for a job at Butlins Holiday Camps. Bognor Regis in Sussex was not my idea of fun!! My father and I had always joked about working at these places, but the reality was slightly different. Built along the lines of a large factory with rows of basic and identical "chalets" and with an impressive wire fence enclosing the complex, it was the very model of all I now abhor of "British holidaying"! I worked as a barman in a huge barn of a "pub". As our licensing hours were 30 minutes earlier and later than the town pubs, there was a veritable stampede at opening time, and the avalanche continued for the rest of the evening. It was truly exhausting and the wages were, I remember, a pittance. The only benefit was the Scandinavian students who came over to work for the summer.

Free as a Bird

My great friend, Clive Vero, and I, in our early youth, had decided that we would eventually become pilots and fly the world's skies. I remember one summer day in 1962 reading the Telegraph, and seeing an advert for the Royal Navy. They were recruiting young men to be pilots on a 5 year commission. This would be my new destiny. My only problem was that I had only four O-levels, and the minimum requirement was five! Mummy, or Mishie[36] as she was now known, saw her original judgement had been vindicated, and stumped up £60 for me to attend a cramming college in Birmingham to achieve my fifth pass in French. By the autumn, armed with my precious certificates, I applied to the Navy recruiting office, and early in the following year, I received instructions to travel to Biggin Hill and Portsmouth for my aptitude tests and, if successful, my Admiralty interviews!

---

[36] *My elder sister, Jenny, had married Mike Griffiths in 1957, and already their children, Sara, Jeremy and Andrew had renamed their grandparents as Mishie and Jim.*

As soon as I arrived at RAF Biggin Hill, and saw the rest of the applicants, my heart sank. They all seemed to be bigger and brighter than myself; just like the sports stars I had seen so often collect their school colours at Oundle. What hope had I?

During the induction process we were prodded, probed and pushed to our limits over the next five days. It was, actually, great fun; particularly when we got down to Portsmouth and HMS Sultan for the naval bit. I enjoyed being given a challenge to get my team of six over an imaginary chasm with only three ropes and a few poles. I managed to give a talk on hat making to an audience of fifty without my left leg twitching too much, and although my final interview with an Admiral and three Captains was certainly intimidating, I felt I had done my best.

The proof of all my unnecessary agitation and insecurity was to arrive in the post one October morning. I was to report to Britannia Naval College in Dartmouth to join the Royal Navy as an Air Cadet. So on the 29th October 1963, I duly arrived by train at Kingswear station with about 20 other rather nervous blokes to be met by a very smart cadet and be escorted across the river Dart on the ferry and driven by truck to the great building sitting proudly on the hill above the town.

Back to School again!

The air cadets were housed in Hawke division, a building detached from the main college. We were only to have two terms at Dartmouth, rather than the seaman cadets, who spent three years in training.[37] However, apart from this distinction, we were all in the same boat – and that, for the first six weeks, meant we were running (literally) from dawn till dusk every day; learning drill, seamanship on the river, knots, naval history, plus all the normal school subjects once again. We were taught Naval etiquette; how to write letters; even how to dance! We were going to be perfect young gentlemen, and instructed in the only way the Navy knew how – the hard way. And so we scampered around in our itchy blue serge tunic, keeping a wary eye out for the nastier Sub Lieutenants who hounded us unmercifully, and saluting anything that moved – just in case. After six weeks, we were eventually deemed fit and proper enough to be allowed to go "ashore", and Naval life began!

Into the Blue

The highlight of my second term at Dartmouth was that glorious first flight. It was February 4th, on a very cold but beautifully clear day. Cadet Stafford walked out towards his aeroplane in a thick kapok flying suit, looking a bit like the Michelin man, his heavy parachute clunking

---

[37] *The middle year was spent serving on a training ship with the Fleet.*

against the back of his legs. His instructor, Mr Brown, explained the pre-flight checks, and then assisted him up into the front seat. Soon, the Gipsy Major engine had clattered into life and we bumped over the grass airfield at Roborough on the outskirts of Plymouth. Airborne, and my instructor took us higher and higher into the deep blue sky until we were 5,000 feet over the city. For thirty minutes we looped and rolled and that was my introduction to flying that wonderful old biplane – the Tiger Moth. At long last, Biggles, my schoolboy hero, and I were as one!

Before long, it was time to pass out of the College. Of the twenty or so entrants, only about twelve of us had managed to survive the course. I was one of the five selected to go "rotary-wing", and so in early June, Midshipman Stafford drove himself in Mishie's Mini[38] to RAF Linton on Ouse in Yorkshire to get down to serious flying training. Here, we completed 75 hours on the little Chipmunk to learn the basic aviation skills. On the 16th July 1964, I went solo for the first time – an experience every pilot always remembers.

It was good fun being on an Air Force station, having a batman look after your daily needs and being in a single bedroom after the enforced communal living at Dartmouth; York was close by, and we had some memorable runs ashore!! It was an idyllic summer, but towards the end of October, it was time to pack my bag and head down to the West Country and RNAS Culdrose[39] on the Lizard peninsula in Cornwall.

A rotary Life

Wow, at last a helicopter. What a difference from a plane with wings. Yes, it still had a sort of joystick and pedals to choose the direction to go, but also a lever in the left hand to go up and down and a throttle on the end of it to power the engine. It was an un-nerving experience to start with, and the similarity with a one-armed paper hanger was not just my imagination!

The little Hiller was a great little helicopter to learn on. It had just two rotor blades, a tail rotor of course, to ensure we didn't spin around the other way, and a Perspex bubble cockpit with just two seats. This was all sitting on a skid undercarriage. My first instructor was Bill Waddell-Wood, an Australian – very patient and great fun to fly with. Culdrose, at that time, was a very busy place. Although primarily the

---

[38] I had somehow managed to borrow this great little car from Mum during my last term at Dartmouth. I remember some very hairy trips around the Devon countryside, including a brilliant Good Friday jaunt to Salcombe, when we managed to get lost driving back, turning left at a ford, and ending up having 5 days punishment for getting back 5 minutes late. But I did meet a fantastic girl!!!
[39] Royal Naval Air Station, also known as HMS Seahawk, as the Navy treats all its shore establishments as though they were a ship.

main Naval Helicopter base, it also was home to a quite a few aeroplanes and you had to be extra vigilant when flying around. For most of our basic training we used to fly off to a small satellite airfield at Predannack, close to the Goonhilly Satellite station which had just opened. This was a fun time, particularly when flying solo; scooting around cumulus clouds, low level flying around the Lizard coast – free as a bird.

Before long, we were getting down to the serious stuff. The Whirlwind had been in service since 1958. It had a great big rotary engine sitting in the nose, and we, the pilots, sat in a cockpit above, between it and a cabin. In its early days, the engine was not very reliable, and this helicopter had a habit of deciding to descend rather abruptly. Fortunately, none of us students knew about this, so we just got on with the job of learning to fly this rather ungainly contraption! We practiced all sorts of manoeuvres; autorotations, winching off Looe Bar, and formation flying.

After 40 hours of this elderly lady, we finally got our hands on the latest helicopter, the Westland Wessex HAS1. This was much more like the real thing. Now we were flying a jet turbine powered, four-bladed monster. At long last, after passing my final handling test, I was awarded my pilot's wings on 16th July 1965, by the Commandant of the Royal Marines, Major General Grant. Two very proud parents watched the ceremony, and, at long last, I felt that I had found my niche in life.

The delights of dipping

By this stage, I had been selected to go to an anti-submarine squadron[40], which meant that once I had passed my operational flying training course at Portland, I would be posted to an Aircraft Carrier. I spent the next three months at Portland Bill, learning the complex manoeuvres involved in detecting and attacking submarines. The Wessex used a sonar system which was deployed by lowering an acoustic device on an 80 foot cable whilst hovering over the sea at thirty feet. This was known as dipping and the device was called the ball – so lots of room for naval humour to be used!

At this time we also started getting very involved in fleet exercises, and the delights of spending time aboard HMS Lofoten[41]. This was a converted tank landing ship, which could "accommodate" two Wessex

---

[40] the alternative being flying the twin-engined variant in a Commando squadron.
[41] It was eventually replaced by a purpose built helicopter support ship – RFA Engadine – during my last year whilst instructing at Portland. Being aboard was bliss, apart from the fact that all the Wardroom stewards were very gay, and had to be addressed by their girlie names!!

helicopters. It was a pig in all ways; awful to land on, dreadful to live in – an experience to remember.

Singapore and the Ark

After two years of training, I finally received orders to proceed to my first ship. This was going to be to Singapore to join HMS Ark Royal and 815 Squadron. I arrived at Paya Libar airport at 4 in the morning, very tired after an endless 3 day trooping flight in an unbearably noisy Britannia aircraft. There was nobody to meet me or instructions on how to get to my squadron. So a very timid and exhausted officer finally arrived at the Dockyard, by taxi, at 6.30 to find this enormous ship stretching into the distance. I found my way to the quarterdeck gangway, introduced myself to the Officer of the Day, only to find that my squadron had been disembarked to an airfield in the middle of the island. However, I was given a hearty breakfast in the Wardroom before being transported to Sembewang.

This was, of course, my first taste of the Orient, and the difference from grey old England could not have been more marked. We were stationed at this wonderful, pre war, Officers Mess at HMS Simbang. Not a lot seemed to have changed since the old colonial days; it was very spacious with tall louvered windows, high ceilings and large fans slowly stirring the tepid air. Local servants served us drinks as we sat in bamboo chairs, and the food was all so different – curries, nasi goring, fresh pineapple – fantastic. Of course, we worked as well; but only in the mornings usually; and as our ship had suffered a major boiler fire, we had plenty of time to see all over the island of Singapore and across the causeway into Johor Bahru and Malaya. I won't bore you with the mundane details, but it was a marvellous and eye-opening initiation for a young man.

In early December, with the ship repaired, we set off – to Fremantle, Australia. This Ark Royal was the fifth ship to bear the illustrious name. She had been laid down during the last stages of the war and launched in 1950, weighing 50,000 tons, she was, with HMS Eagle, our largest ship afloat. Aboard were 1,700 sailors spread over ten decks and finding my way around was a major expedition. Apart from the vast hangars to store the aircraft and helicopters, there were innumerable sailor's messes, storerooms, briefing rooms, laundries, canteens and even a Chinese tailor and a shoemaker.

Before long we were flying on submarine screening exercises with the various support frigates and destroyers; flying night planeguard for the aircraft being launched and recovered, and transferring mail and personnel to other ships in the task force. I remember flying as co-pilot with George Barras, the Senior Pilot,[42] into Perth to land the liaison officers for our visit. Then the ship was docking and virtually all the ship's crew were being whisked away on hospitality visits to stay with Australian families for Christmas. I have never known such generosity, and their kindness has always endeared the Aussies to me.

Being on the beach on Christmas day was a fantastic experience; the sand so hot that bare feet were burning. I booked a phone call home and remember having to pay some £12 for a 5 minute call – very expensive in those days.

1966 and the Beira patrol

Soon it was back to Singapore, looking forward very much to a visit to Hong Kong and Japan. From a personal point of view, the world was relatively safe at that time. We had just finished the Indonesian confrontation; the Cold War with the Soviet Union was, of course, still a very large issue; and the Vietnam War was growing in intensity for the United States; but, actually, for the British, the only trouble-spots were localised, and didn't require the services of a large carrier task force. So life was fun, relaxed and safe!

Unfortunately for us, just prior to the ship departing for more exotic ports, the newly elected Prime Minister of Rhodesia, Ian Smith, declared independence from the Commonwealth, and incurred the wrath of the Labour Government, led by Prime Minister Harold Wilson. Before long we were sent off to the East Coast of Africa to initiate an oil embargo to force the white Rhodesians to the conference table.

On the way there, somewhere near Gan in the Maldive Islands, I experienced my first "knee-trembler". I was flying co-pilot to the squadron C.O., John Kelly, and we were doing a night exercise some 10 miles from the ship. Whilst we were in the hover, with the sonar ball in the sea, there was suddenly a very loud bang, and a blast of flame from the exhaust. Very quickly we got all the gear in, and started flying towards the ship. Meanwhile the Ark, having received our emergency call, steamed at maximum speed towards us. The Boss decided to keep the helicopter low and slow in case the engine packed up and we had to ditch. Every minute or so, there was another rumble, bang and spout of flame, before, after 10 minutes or so, we managed to get back on the flight deck. The engineers pronounced a main engine bearing failure and a very lucky crew to have got the aircraft back and remain dry!

For 70 odd days we sailed up and down the Mozambique channel, investigating the occasional tanker, and getting thoroughly bored. Our only consolation was a week in Mombasa, where I learned to water-ski

---

[42] *SP for short and second in command of the squadron*

in the harbour. After numerous tumbles, I eventually became reasonably proficient; but was horrified to be told afterwards that this stretch of water was a regular shark breeding ground!

I also managed a weekend in Nairobi, travelling there by steam train. It was a marvellous trip, rattling over the veldt, seeing elephant and giraffe ambling along, and being looked after in the proper colonial style. I made a point of having a large gin and tonic at the Stanley Hotel in the middle of the city, watching the Hemingway type characters setting off on their safaris. As I was idly eyeing up the "tottie", a Mini car screamed to a halt by the pavement, and a familiar face came towards me – it was Sandy Birkbeck, last seen at Oundle, who now was a coffee trader there. "Could I come to a wedding up near Mount Kenya?" – like a shot, I was packed into the Mini, and off we set for a 140 mile trek into the bush. My feet never touched the ground; Rhodesians are a lovely bunch and, boy, could they party. Early on Monday morning, I was deposited back; very much the worse for wear, at the dockside in Mombasa, only just in time to catch the ship on her way back to Singapore – phew!

Home to Guzz

In May we finally left the Mozambique Channel after our second patrol there, and steamed towards Aden and the Suez Canal. This was another exciting experience, particularly being on such a large warship, which seemed almost too big for the channel. The political relationship with Egypt at that time were none too cordial, and at one point we were buzzed for about an hour by two jet aircraft: this became quite amusing when one of them had some kind of problem and crashed in the desert a little way from the canal. In Alexandria, we were invaded by "gully-gully"[43] men and various souvenir sellers so we could stock up on goodies to take home. Then it was a sail across the Mediterranean, calling briefly at Malta and Gibraltar before a final dash up the Channel to Plymouth, arriving there with all pomp and ceremony in June. Mishie and Jim had travelled down to meet the ship and it was wonderful to see them, and for me to show them over my home! I know that they were hugely impressed by the ship and seeing their son as a fully fledged naval officer. It was lovely seeing green England again and the prospect of three weeks leave.

Here come the Yanks

In July, it was back to Culdrose for more operational training before once more joining the Ark for a trip up to the north of Norway for a

---

[43] *An Egyptian magician, mostly playing the three cup, one ball, trick*

large NATO exercise. Although the British task force was impressive, it was totally overwhelmed when the American 6th Fleet arrived at the rendezvous. There were three enormous aircraft carriers, many escort vessels and even a battleship, with more aircraft and helicopters than one could imagine. After a week of sustained around the clock tactical exercising, it was a fantastic to arrive in Oslo for a welcome break. We had a number of American ships there as well, and before long the Yanks were over with us for a great party. American warships were, by tradition, always "dry". The Royal Navy, thank goodness, never had any of that nonsense. Whilst I was serving, the ratings still received their daily rum ration, and as "Officer of the Watch", it was my occasional duty to supervise the allocation, usually from a very large oak tub – pusser's rum was 90 proof and it was a heady experience to stand over many gallons of neat spirit on a hot day!

Meeting the Queen Mum

In early September 1966, we embarked for what was to be our last trip on the dear old "Ark". Although she was ancient, noisy and extremely hot to live in, she had a lovely aura about her and was a very happy ship. She had been launched by Queen Elizabeth, the Queen Mother, in 19 and Her Majesty had always kept a close relationship with the ship, and so as we approached Aberdeen, she came on board to inspect the ship. On that day I was squadron Duty Officer and so was presented to HRH when she looked over our helicopter. This was the first of a number of royal introductions I was fortunate to receive over the years..

Playing Commandos

With the Ark Royal being de-commissioned for a major refit, it had been decided that 815 Squadron would also be retired. However, for the last ten days we were allowed to play soldiers; our helicopters were painted in camouflage colours, and the eight aircraft set off to a mock war that started in Catterick in Yorkshire, moved over to South Wales and ended on Salisbury Plain. After a number of embarrassing errors due to poor map reading (we were flying at very low levels!); I think it was decided that the Navy were better dunking their balls in the sea, rather than making a "balls-up" overland. My final act in the squadron was to ensure that our mascot, the Harp[44], was transported to the Fleet Air Arm Museum at Yeolvilton for safe keeping.

820 and the Margaree

After three weeks leave, it was back to Culdrose and my new squadron. 820 were flying the Wessex HAS1 as well, so nothing changed except the personnel. Our boss was Tony Casdagli, a great pilot and a real gentleman, who I had first met during my initial helicopter training on 705 Squadron. Already I had moved up the seniority ladder, with quite a few less experienced pilots joining the squadron too.

Almost immediately, the Senior Pilot, Colin Moorcraft, and I was sent off to join a Canadian destroyer, HMCS Margaree, on another large exercise taking place to the north of Scotland. Although I had made a number of deck landings on smaller ships, this was the first time I had been deployed for a longer period. Late November is not, I have to tell you, the best time to be on a relatively small ship off the coast of Cape Wrath!

It certainly lived up to its name, and for three weeks we tossed and turned, including a force 10 storm, trying to fly operations off such a wildly moving helicopter deck. It didn't help one morning, when I was on the bridge, watching the inclinometer turn past 40 degrees, to be told that the ship was designed to roll right over. I think they were taking the "piss" – but I'm still not really sure.

The highlight of that trip, for me, was one miserable morning, with a very low cloud base of 200 feet. We couldn't fly, but we were told to expect an imminent air attack. I shall never forget the sight, without any forewarning, of a Vulcan bomber, emerging out of the clag at 150 feet above us, and then turning on full afterburners and blasting back up into the heavens – majestic!

In December, we installed ourselves at RAF Valley in Anglesey for a week's Mountain flying course. Having spent so long flying across endless miles of ocean, it was an extraordinary experience to be whirling around steep valleys and gusting air currents with unpredictable weather conditions. Trying to maintain straight and level flight with no obvious horizon is particularly difficult, and I have always had great respect for those who fly helicopters in the hills.

---

[44] *For whatever reason, I had been appointed "Harp Officer", which entailed a weekly clean of a large orchestral harp which was kept on the ship next door to the Captain's cabin. Because of this association, we also received from time to time a goodly supply of Guinness!!*

Lieutenant R.N.

After Christmas, it was back to Culdrose, but this time with two rings on my sleeves. Being promoted to Lieutenant was not, I should add, a reward for great and good service; but rather just the normal progression of promotion.

It was around this time that in January 1967 that I first met Sally Richards, who eventually was to be my first wife. I had acquired, by this time, a second-hand MGB sports car. It was very flash, a two tone grey with a soft top. One evening, I was driving through Helston towards Porthleven with my great buddy, Brian Palmer, when we spotted two nice looking girls walking down Meneage Street. We thought a little chat-up was in order, and before long we had them squeezed into the car and were roaring off to the Atlantic Inn.

Sally and I got on really well; she had a great sense of slightly off-beat humour and was very attractive. The only problem I found out a little later was that she was not yet sixteen. Ooops. Well, I suppose I had no excuses then or now, but at the time it just seemed a natural thing to be going out together, even if the rules said NO.

In early February, we had a fortnight's deployment to Ballykelly in Northern Ireland. Although there had been problems with the IRA for some years, it was still fairly low key, and nothing like the problems our troops encountered in the 1970's and 80's. Part of our offshore training was conducted on an old Tank Landing Craft called HMS Lofoten. It could take two Wessex on its modified deck, but it was a pig to land on, and great care had to be taken to avoid the superstructure at the bow and stern.

In March, I was elected to undertake an Instrument Rating Instructors course. This was a great honour as only the best pilots were taken on for this demanding standard; but the experience I gained stood me in good stead for the reminder of my flying career and got me out of a few scrapes. In the meantime, I was preparing for a scrape of a different nature. By this time I had rented a tiny cottage in Helston and Sally and I had settled into a comfortable but secretive relationship.

In mid June, the Squadron finally embarked on HMS Eagle in preparation for her next operational tour to the Far East. Having completed all the necessary readiness inspections and exercises, we set sail in late August for Cape Town. We spent a week there in early September, and again we enjoyed tremendous hospitality including, for myself, a weekend stay with a local family, the De Toits. It was, of course, still a very Afrikaans government and apartheid was very evident with the segregation of the black and coloured communities. The ship acted as a giant night club with all of Capetowns high society converging on us.

Towards the end of that week, an even more memorable and earth shattering event occurred when I received, out of the blue, a letter from Sally saying she was pregnant and expecting our baby in December. It was one of those "stand still" moments when the whole world seems to be sitting on you. I had, of course, absolutely no forewarning of this event. Even worse, there seemed to be nobody to whom I could go to and discuss my predicament. In the event, I consigned the news to myself alone, and was not to disclose it to anyone for another 15 months.

For the remainder of that year, the Eagle steamed across to Singapore and around the Far East, and then in November back to Aden to cover the final withdrawal of the British troops who had been garrisoned there. The internal situation had been getting progressively worse, and it was finally decided that its strategic importance was no longer significant. In my Naval career, this was the only time we were given weapons to use. Each of us had a service revolver, and a machine gun was carried in the cockpit. One or two helicopters were shot at, but luckily no real damage was caused. On November 20th, my last trip with 820 Squadron was to carry Sir Humphrey Trevelyan, the High Commissioner and Admiral LeFanu, the Fleet commander from Command Hill in Aden to the ship. The next day I left on one of the last trooping flights back to Cyprus and then home to England.

The last stretch and a big blast

In mid January 1968, I reported for duty at RNAS Portland to join 737 Squadron as an operational Instructor. This was the normal situation for an officer on a five year commission. After the hurly burly life aboard ship, this was a much more sedate experience. Together with two other Instructors, Mike Fuller and Nigel Thornton, I shared a lovely little rose bedecked cottage near Weymouth. The work was rather repetitive as we took new arrivals from Culdrose through all the sequence of anti-submarine exercises.

In February, I returned to Culdrose for a conversion on to the Wessex Mark 3 – in many ways similar to the Mark 1, but with a much more powerful sonar and an area radar. On one particular morning I was summoned to the base Captains office. I was marched in to salute a very stern looking gentleman, who proceeded to give me a huge dressing-down for my unlawful relationship with a fifteen year old girl. The shit had truly hit the fan. In the event I was banned from going anywhere near Porthleven although at that point the last thing on my mind was to get involved with the Richards family.

Back to Portland and a lovely summer. I was due to leave the Navy at the end of September, and amazingly enough, after my recent blasting for "conduct unbecoming an Officer", I was offered a General

List commission; in effect, a long term career. But by then, I think I had had enough of Oily Cues, as the term "Officer Like Qualities" was known; and the lure of commercial aviation and loads of money was too much to pass by. Before I left at the end of September, I was even allowed to go down to Culdrose for a quick refresher and type rating test on the little Hiller 12E to qualify for my commercial licence – good old Navy!!

Over the years, I've often wondered in those few life changing decisions - "what if". What if I had accepted that offer, where would my career have taken me. My Senior Pilot on 820, Ben Bathurst, was to become First Sea Lord and the very last Admiral of the Fleet. Two of my observers, Dave Dobson and Chris Craig became Admirals as well, and many of those who stayed the course retired as Captains or Commanders – complete with a very nice index-linked pensions. But that was then, and now I had to go out and face the world.

Bristow's, a Birthday and a Marriage

Prior to leaving the RN, I had been offered a job by Bristow Helicopters, a company based at Redhill Aerodrome in Sussex and which, at that time, operated over 70 helicopters around the world; nearly all engaged in oil drilling support operations. Before I could join them, I had to gain my commercial licence, and this was achieved at Oxford Airport, close to where Jenny, Mike and family where living, in Yarnton in a lovely house called Mead Farm.

Early December found me at Westland Helicopters in Yeovil with my old pal, Brian Palmer, doing a ground course on the Whirlwind Series 3[45]. One night in the bar, thinking very much of the impending first birthday of my son, Matthew; I told Brian all about the last fifteen months and the agonies of conscience I had been going through. He was the first person in all that time that I had been able to confide in. Despite all the hassle from the Navy and with very minor contact from the Richards family, I really wanted to see this little boy. After quite a few brain and emotion loosening pints, I decided to drive down that weekend and take the plunge.

I rang Sally and arranged a meeting at Penmount[46] on December 13th, his first birthday. It started as an emotional affair, but somehow it became the most natural of reunions, and both Sally's parents, Jack and Mona, were very welcoming. I had brought some toys for Matthew, and

---

[45] A jet turbine powered version of the old Whirlwind I had trained on initially at Culdrose.

[46] the Richards family home in Porthleven. Father, Jack, worked at the torpedo trials unit at Culdrose; whilst mother, Mona, did summer B&B's. Younger brother, John, was to become a world famous tenor using the name John Treleaven.

it was wonderful to meet him after the trauma we had all suffered during that period.

Somehow or other, I ended my short stay with a marriage proposal. It wasn't planned, it wasn't actually to do with my conscience, but it was just so good having a little family around me. My next task was to go home to Witherley, and tell my dear, long suffering parents, that not only were they to have a daughter-in-law, but also, a new grandson! They were, in a word, brilliant. My father said he had already guessed something was up (because of letters forwarded for maintenance payments) but even so, to accept such a surprise, with the good heart they displayed, was fantastic!

So on 18th January 1969, we were married at the little church in Porthleven. We spent our very short honeymoon in a little third floor flat in St Ives. It was very cold and filled with damp nappies, but it was so different and so domesticated that I remember it still with great affection.

Despite my new status, Bristow's had little mercy, and on January 20th, I was starting my new commercial pilots' life at Redhill, doing a conversion to the Whirlwind. My initial two year contract was either going to be Nigeria, or alternatively to Kharg Island in the Persian Gulf. Both, I learnt, were pretty dire postings. In the meantime, it was off to Great Yarmouth for my first taste of the North Sea oil business. After some of the flying I had done in the Navy, such as landing on a rolling and wallowing ship, the oil platform helidecks seemed to be pretty sedate.

In the middle of February, I was told that all had changed and I was off to Trinidad instead. Oh what joy – a Caribbean island instead of the sweat and misery of the initiation postings. I was very lucky, although it was achieved through an unfortunate hard landing and injury to an old naval mate out there. And with it, the added pleasure of flying the JetRanger, a smart 5 seater, which had just entered service. After an amazing 3 hour conversion and a quick type rating exam, it was off to Port of Spain, leaving my poor wife and small son, now renamed Toby, behind.

Rum Punch and Carnival

Trinidad was certainly different to cold and wet Cornwall. We were based at Mayaro on the east coast in a small tin hangar that could just squeeze in our two helicopters, a Whirlwind[47] with fixed floats and the small JetRanger which was moved around on a large trolley. The

---

[47] *The Whirlwind had a single Gnome turbine engine, carrying 8 passengers, whilst the smaller Bell 206 Jetranger could carry four.*

floating rig, Bluewater 3, was drilling only about 30 miles offshore, and so flights were both short and infrequent.

Bristow's had a policy that wives could only come out on contract after six months, so during that time I stayed at the strangest hotel, the Mayaro Beach. It was run by a small tubby Portuguese, and was built in what can best be described as Miami Hemingway – that is Spanish American in a very run down style. We seemed to live mostly on goat meat, and because there was a lot of mangrove swamps behind the beach, I was consumed in turn by squadrons of ravenous mosquitoes.

Other than these minor inconveniences, life was sweet – apart from missing my new family. However, that was corrected in August, and we settled down to an idyllic existence in a rented beach house. This was our introduction to the expatriate life. A tax free salary paid into a Bermuda bank account, a live in maid, and really just a long holiday, with a little work thrown in occasionally!

Towards the end of January 1970, another rig joined the hunt for oil, and as a consequence, a new hangar was built in Port of Spain, the capital, on the western side of the island. We now had another helicopter, more pilots and a heavier work schedule. We also left our little bit of heaven and rented a bungalow in the northern part of the city, close to the Country Club.

This was much more puckah – a throwback to the old colonial days. Here we had a lovely maid, called Merle, and before long I had taken on a brown spotted Dalmatian and a green parrot. Unfortunately Moses, the dog, soon disposed of the parrot, so I invested in a macaw, called Merlin. He was a beautiful bird, and we eventually got him to talk a little. Although I clipped a wing to stop him flying away, he still managed to escape on the odd occasion, but somehow or other he always came home.

In February we had our first taste of Carnival. For two weeks beforehand, the city was throbbing to the sounds exploding from the calypso tents and the parties that seemed to happen almost every night. A great deal of rum was consumed and we began to feel truly Trinidadian. In those days, the steel band was an amazing experience, and the melodies seemed to go on and on in our heads for weeks afterwards. On carnival Tuesday we all trooped down to the Savannah to watch the Bands perform, and I doubt whether I have ever seen such a glittering spectacle in my life since.

But Trinidad is also a very volatile place, with its exotic mix of negroes, Indians, Chinese and whites, and in July there was the excitement of a genuine rebellion. It transpired that a group of dissident soldiers had mutinied at their base at Chaguramas west of Port of Spain.

They had set off towards the city with a plan to capture and, allegedly, hang the senior government ministers. Very luckily, the miniscule Trinidad Navy, with one of its two gunboats, under the command of a British officer, fired at the rebel's convoy and halted their advance on the coast road. Rumours persisted that this conspiracy had the support of Cuba, and so whilst the whole of the island was put under a 24 hour curfew, our helicopters were to fly surveillance missions to spot gunrunners along the coast.

Around Christmas, my parents and Angie came out to stay. I remember having to do a Santa Claus run with the larger helicopter to various schools in Port of Spain and San Fernando, and Mum came for the flight, and was highly amused to be delivering a black Father Christmas on such a hot day! In February 1971, we enjoyed our second carnival, and then it was time to go home. It had been a memorable experience for us all, and it was so sad to leave, particularly the animals, although we found good homes for Moses and Merlin.

A Holiday and a big Adventure

Whilst Toby stayed with Jack and Mona in Cornwall, Sally and I went off on a motoring holiday around Holland, Luxembourg and France. It was a great break and made up a little for our so-short honeymoon two years earlier. It was reasonably uneventful until our last night in Paris, when we decided to push the boat out and eat at Maxims.

In those days, before credit cards, cash was king; and we had carefully worked out what we could spend. However, when the bill came, my wallet was somewhat short of the required amount! Unbelievably, Sally had to stay at the restaurant as a sort of hostage, whilst I rushed back to the hotel to bring back our remaining store of traveller's cheques – how embarrassing was that?

Back at Bristow's in Redhill, I succeeded again in securing a great posting – this time it was to be an onshore drilling operation, working for a French company, Total, in Indonesia. The best bit was that our base would be in Singapore, working a two week on, one week at home routine. The even better bit was that we were to fly one of the Wessex helicopters all the way out there from England – a mammoth, but truly exciting ferry flight!

But first I had to do a quick Wessex Mk 60 conversion, not a real problem as I had many hours already on the single engine Naval version, whilst this type had two engines. Again, my luck seemed to be with the gods, for I was flown out to Las Palmas for three weeks to get a few hours in.

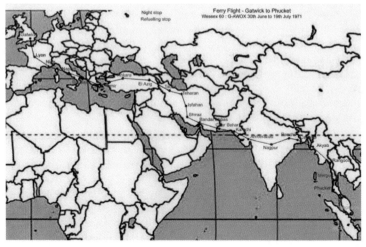

On June 30th, we finally set off from Redhill on what was planned as a two week flight to Singapore. John Hobday, being senior to me was the aircraft Captain and we flew most of the trip down to India swopping seats; although when we got into the really nasty weather, I seemed to do most of the flying!!

In the cabin we also had Nick Owen, a bearded engineer who was not only very talented but also good company. After clearing customs at Gatwick, we set off across the Channel for our first night stop at Lyon. However bad weather forced us to make an unscheduled landing at Chateauneuf – a great start to our trip. The helicopter had been fitted with a cabin fuel tank to cope with some of the longer legs, and on a couple of occasions, we had to shut down one engine to conserve fuel which enabled us to fly for 4 ½ hours.

From Lyon, we flew on to Naples, Athens, Izmir, El Azig[48], Tabriz and Teheran. Navigation in those days was almost medieval compared with modern day sat-nav. We had an ADF, a basic VOR/ILS system and VHF and HF radio. There was no autopilot, it was hands on all the way, and when we were out of range of the usual navigation aids, we were back to following a map!

On the leg from El Azig to Tabriz we were transiting the high mountains bordering Iran, and uncomfortably close to the Russian border. Of course, this was at a time when the Cold War was at its peak, and naturally at this critical point we got lost; the road we were following just seemed to disappear. Expecting at any moment to be

---

[48] *Tucked away in the east of Turkey, El Azig was like going back a hundred years or so, with horse drawn carts clattering along the one street outside our basic hotel.*

buzzed by a pair of Mig 21s, we held our nerve and after 20 minutes recovered our route and slid down a long valley into Tabriz.

After a two day break in Teheran, where Bristow's had a big base, we set off again into the dusty brown lunar landscape of the Persian plain and the southern mountains. Isfahan, Shiraz and Bandar Abbas passed by as the temperatures soared. We flew high to keep cool, and out of the heat haze. On our last leg before Karachi, we had to make a refuelling stop at Char Behar. This was used by Imperial Airways in the thirties on the long runs down to the Far East, and amazingly there was still a small depot stocking cans of aviation quality kerosene. Our problem was that there was no-one to refuel us. So for two hours in temperatures of around 40 degrees centigrade, we poured can after can into the aircraft tanks. I seem to remember a figure of 112. Whatever it was, it was one of the most uncomfortable afternoons I have ever spent. Even worse, after that, was another 3 $\frac{1}{2}$ hours flight to Pakistan, stinking of kerosine.

After 3 days in Karachi at a blissfully proper hotel, we set off again on July 13th to Ahmadabad in India. Here we refuelled and cleared customs. This was an experience in itself as it seemed to take forever and I have never seen so many dusty old files surrounding the office walls – it looked as though nothing had been thrown away since the Raj.

Our next night stop was at a small airport near Nagpur. We were taken by a rickety taxi to a very seedy looking hotel in the town, and although it was the best there, we spent the whole night scratching ourselves. The next day, the weather we feared most had arrived. It was now the monsoon season, with incredibly vigorous weather systems bringing violent rainstorms almost every day. We had to spend another night at Nagpur for the weather to clear, staying this time in a sort of rest room at the airport, and living off boiled eggs, the only food that looked edible.

Our next leg was to Calcutta with a stop at Ranchi. However the weather intervened again and we were forced to make a precautionary landing in a jungle area near Khunti to wait for the low clouds to clear. We shut down the engines and looked around at a deserted grassy area surrounded by what seemed to be banana trees – not a soul to be seen.

Within ten minutes, however, the helicopter was surrounded by native Indians peering at this apparition from the skies! They shielded themselves from the torrential rain with these huge leaves, and the women were bare-breasted; more native than I had expected in modern India. We managed after an hour to get airborne again to Ranchi. Thirty years later I discovered that my Uncle Peter was buried in Ranchi War Cemetery, having been sadly killed when his aircraft had crashed in bad weather in the same area. What strange twists and turns life plays on us.

In Calcutta, we were gratefully taken by a BOAC aircrew bus into the city centre to spend the night in a luxurious hotel. Walking out into the street was totally fascinating. This was the year of the Bangladesh revolution and thousands upon thousands of refugees from East Pakistan had descended on the city, sleeping on the streets and in the parks. It was quite literally a seething mass of humanity interspersed with the sacred cows and an incredible colophony of hooting from countless cars and lorries.

The next day, we had to get back to Dum-Dum Airport, but this time only in a local taxi. Getting to one of the ring roads, we found our way barred by a mass of striking workers. A heated argument with our taxi driver ensued, and at one point John wanted us to leave the car. However Nick and I vetoed that idea and virtually threatened the driver with instant death if he didn't get the taxi through the melee. This seemed to work and we managed to get away.

Leaving Calcutta and flying across the Ganges delta we ran into even more extreme weather. To avoid the worst storms we headed towards an airport in Burma called Akyab. Although we had negotiated visas to enter Burma with great difficulty, these were issued specifically for Rangoon, and to land elsewhere created a certain amount of official pandemonium! We were taken to spend the night in a government rest hut, under armed guard, and hurriedly put back on our helicopter the next morning.

Unfortunately, the weather had got no better, and for the next three hours I flew the Wessex in the worst thunderstorms I have ever known. We were flying in very turbulent cloud, in incredibly heavy rain and with no navigation aids! It was pure dead reckoning, hoping we were just off the coast; not daring to climb any higher, and very aware that just inland was higher ground than our 1000 foot altitude!

One further and rather sobering consideration was our technical situation. Since leaving Karachi, we had been required to do a specific and complicated check on the rotor hub. This is an alloy casting which carried the four main rotor blades.

There had been apparently a fatal accident, where part of the head had disintegrated and a rotor blade had detached in flight. This was not good news, as a four bladed helicopter does not fly very well with only three rotor blades. In order to complete the maintenance check we had to do a dye penetrant test to see whether there were any cracks in this component. This was an almost impossible task in the weather we had been experiencing. So our fingers were very crossed and our anus's very tight as we bucked and tossed in the stormy monsoon.

Obviously our luck held out, and we reached Rangoon to spend an extraordinary night in the most wonderful colonial hotel – The Rangoon Palace. I think we must have been the only guests as tourists to Burma in those days were heavily discouraged by the authorities. It was enormous, with a remembrance of that languid air that Forster and Kipling brought to their novels.

The flowing day we set off for the last two legs of our journey. In Phucket in Thailand, we were able at last to carry out the maintenance test on the main rotor assembly, and, believe it or not, we had a hairline crack in one of the arms.

So that was it, the helicopter was grounded. We sent a memorable telex message to Redhill " G-AWOX is f****d in Phucket"!! As we boarded a commercial flight down to Singapore, we reflected on a marvellous experience which covered over 7,500 miles in 20 days and 76 hours of flying.

A Jungle Life for me

In Singapore, the team of pilots and engineers who were going to start the Djambi contract gathered. We had two Wessex Mk 60 helicopters that the Company had bought from the Brunei Defence Force, and had been overhauled at Seletar airfield. However, it was not until mid September that we managed to get the aircraft and all our equipment into Sumatra and prepare for the start of the operation.

Meanwhile, Sally and Toby had flown out from England and we had rented a nice bungalow near Nee Soon, a little way out from the city centre. I was fairly used to the oriental life from my Navy days, but Sally was fascinated by the colours and smells and bustle of the native Chinese, Malays and Indians. We were inundated by the local shops all trying to be our favoured supplier. We had also hired a maid, and she took over running the kitchen and looking after Toby if we were out. Every week, the grocer would arrive and supply what we needed, and later at Christmas we even received a free box of goodies to show their appreciation of our patronage. England – eat your heart out!

But after almost two months of idleness, it was back to flying and a totally new experience. Our task was to fly all the drilling rig components, supplies and men from site to site in the Sumatran jungle. The maximum load that the Wessex could carry on the hook slung underneath it was 4,600 pounds. So every bit of the rig had to be dismantled to be less than that figure. It was a daunting task, and in the end, I remember that the whole rig including the accommodation portacabins was about 1,700 separate loads. Added to that figure were all the drilling pipes and other consumables needed to operate the drilling programme; possibly altogether over 3,000 trips.

We were based in a hangar by the side of a large river in Djambi, a large city in the centre of Sumatra. The river was used to transport all the materials to the closest point to the rig site. A team of locals led by a wiry little Frenchman (ex Foreign Legion) went by foot into the jungle and cleared a big enough site for us to hover the helicopter in with more labourers. The area was then cleared so that we had enough space for all the equipment to be brought in by underslung loads. Our first rig site was 32 kilometres from the river, quite a bit further than we had been advised, and because of the extra fuel we needed, flying the loads out was particularly demanding, as the poor old Gnome turbine engines struggled to provide enough power!

The aircraft were flying 10 hours a day, virtually continuously. We flew with just one pilot doing about $2\frac{1}{4}$ hours at a go, and then a similar break. After a fortnight on the operation we flew back to Singapore for a week's rest. It was really hard work, but very satisfying to see the rig grow in the middle of virgin jungle. In a way, it was also sad to see modern industrial demands spoil such wonderful and diverse untouched countryside.

Occasionally, we took the recce crew up river for them to walk into the jungle to find the next site. I remember once landing by a small village and waiting for an hour or two whilst the oil crew discussed a new rig location with the local headman. It was obvious that none of the villagers had ever seen a helicopter before. Very gradually they approached us, terribly afraid it might attack them, and then began to touch it and run away just in case it bit them. Before long, they were rubbing their bodies along the fuselage as though the magic would flow into them! At this point we got rather worried that fifty or so natives would start damaging the aircraft so we had to drive them away to a safer distance. It was quite an experience.

Meanwhile in Singapore, our weeks together were a delight. It was the early days of the tourist and business explosion there, and hotels were leaping up everywhere. Our favourite was the Shangri-La, to which we would go for dinner on my first evening back, perhaps followed by a trip down to Bugis Street to see the seamier side of the night-life.

We had applied for membership of the Tanglin, the most exclusive country club on the island, been interviewed, and accepted; and then enjoyed wonderful days by the pool, being waited on with cool drinks and hot curries. Toby had started school, we had a lovely bunch of neighbours, and life was a dream.

However, on Monday, March 13th (and lucky not to be a Friday), our bubble burst. I was flying a load of fuel drums back to the main rig site on my own, but with a couple of local lads in the cabin. The drums were in a net underneath the helicopter. For a week or so, we had noticed that this particular aircraft was a bit juddery, particularly feeling a vibration through the rudder pedals.

The engineers had checked it out and found no mechanical problems, and we thought it might just be dust getting into some of the controls and giving a little roughness, but not dangerous.

In fact, as I only found quite recently, during a maintenance overhaul undertaken a couple of weeks before, a bonding strip had been incorrectly fitted around an intermediate gearbox on the tail rotor drive shaft[49]. So on this occasion as I pulled in power to hover over the large fuel dump to drop my load, the shaft snapped, and the helicopter, very suddenly and violently, began to turn.

I was in an awful situation. I couldn't climb away, and I dare not land on top of 150 drums of kerosene. So that we continued to rotate, getting quicker and quicker. All the people working at the rig site had now heard the whining and clatter of the engines and knew something awful was happening. After 22 turns, I saw we had moved a few yards away from the dump, and decided that I had to get the helicopter down. With an enormous crash and judder, I pushed down the collective lever and the rotor blades tore into the tree trunks and debris around us.

Amazingly, the aircraft stayed upright, probably held there by the load underneath that I had unsuccessfully tried to jettison. Even more luckily, nothing exploded and there was no fire. A bevy of very energetic French riggers clambered up to the cockpit and wrenched me out, possibly inflicting the only injuries I suffered – a couple of fractured ribs. My gods were smiling on me again that day!

On to the Casbah

Thankfully, I was spared on that occasion; but the accident brought to an abrupt end our idyll in Singapore. Due to a spate of other incidents, some of them due to pilot error, the Indonesian authorities were being particularly difficult; and so it was decided that I would be posted to a small offshore operation in Iran. It was very sad to leave all

---

[49] *Although I was absolutely sure the accident was due to a technical fault, it was only recently that I discovered the true cause from Nigel Corrigan, one of the Djambi engineers,. On a recent maintenance check, the earth bonding around the intermediate tail drive shaft gearbox had been changed. Instead of wrapping the copper bonding wire around 180º, it had been connected straight over, thus creating an uneven force on the supporting bearings. This explained the vibrations pilots had been experiencing for a few hours before the crash. I was the unlucky guy to be there when the drive shaft came apart. To their shame, Bristow's never informed me of the accident investigation findings after the aircraft had been shipped back to Farnborough*

our friends on the island, but towards the end of May, we set off to a very different life in Teheran.

In those days, Iran was still ruled by the Shah and his family. It was much westernised, particularly in the capital, and we expatriates enjoyed a reasonably privileged existence. It was all very busy, noisy and colourful, and Sally, the artist, enjoyed it all from the start.

I was working down on the Persian Gulf at a small town called Bushehr. It was extremely basic, and our fortnight on duty was spent in a local hotel, or meeting up with some other British blokes manning a Decca navigation transmitter nearby. The flying was minimal; the jack-up rig we were servicing was only about 30 minutes flying away, and we were averaging about 25 hours a month on the small 5 seater Bell JetRanger.

It was generally very hot and almost always very boring! The only excitement I remember in the year I was there was when a new crane arrived at the base. Iranians always seem to get rather excited and therefore careless at such times, and sadly two of the local lads holding on to the drilling pipes they were moving got electrocuted when the jib hit an overhead cable.

That evening the camp Boss approached me at supper, and with a certain trepidation wondered whether I could fly the bodies up to Abadan. I politely declined when told that as they had no coffins would it be okay to strap them into the rear seats for the two hour night trip!

Meanwhile in Teheran, Sally and Toby were entertaining both sets of parents who had come to stay. We had found a small house to rent in the north part of the city. It had high walls and a very dirty swimming pool, but was handy for local shops.

My first job was to drain the pool to give it a good clean up. This took many dives and some heavy underwater exertion before I managed to undo the plug at the deep end.

My sister, Angie, visited soon afterwards, and we managed to cadge a lift on the company jeep which was being taken down to Bushehr. This was the very interesting as we spent three days travelling through the fascinating vistas of Isfahan, Persepolis and Shiraz. But, it was very different to our previous postings, and I confess to never really enjoying the Muslim way of life.

A parting of the ways

In May 1973, my posting was coming to an end. So to, unfortunately, was our marriage. The constant separation and differences between our preferred lifestyles had created a growing barrier between us. Sally announced that she would stay on in Teheran for a few months and then make her way home alone, whilst Toby and I returned back to England for our three months leave.

It was a very sad time and I remember a huge sense of bereavement and hollowness for the first twelve months of our separation. To our credit, we have retained a degree of contact and friendship over the years and I think our young son was not too affected by that trauma of a broken marriage as he grew up.

A Danish Smorgasbord

In the middle of September, after a bit of re-familiarisation on the Wessex in Wales and Yarmouth, I set off on my own across a gloomy North Sea to my next posting. The first attempt was abandoned due to poor visibility, but later that day after a 3 hour trip, I landed at Esbjerg Airport on the west coast of Denmark. This was to be my home for the next ten months, and I confess that for a new born bachelor, there couldn't have been a better situation to revive my flagging spirits!

The work was relatively easy; one helicopter, two pilots, and most days spent on an accommodation barge next to the Dan platform being constructed an hour's flying from the airport. Back to the hotel in the evening and then a wander around the lively bars and dance halls of the town. And, of course, those beautiful Danish girls; seemingly ignored by the local men (a typical Viking attitude) and loving the courteous attention of the blue eyed English pilot!

An executive interlude

I think I could have stayed there forever. I fell in love repeatedly, wrote some great poetry, and drank a lot of lager. But the operation came to an end in July 1974, and I had a big decision to make. Bristow's were offering another overseas posting – possibly to Nigeria, but I had reached my saturation point.

Believe it or not, at that precise point, an old Naval mate, Tony Dando, rang me up to find out if I would be interested in an executive flying position in England. He had just joined a small company owned by a multi-millionaire property developer by the name of Charles Mackenzie-Hill. Apart from three jets, they had just bought a Bolkow 105 helicopter and required a second pilot to operate it. I went along to an interview with the owner and his flight Manager at his home near Stoney Stratford, and by the middle of August was doing a short conversion and wearing a smart new uniform.

The helicopter was based at Charles' home, Cosgrove Hall. He was an affable guy, and we seemed to hit it off together very well. Most of the flying was either down to Battersea Heliport on the river Thames in London, or to take the Boss to various country places where he could indulge his passions for hunting or polo. Occasionally, we also undertook charter work, particularly aerial filming.

The Manager was a crazy Polish ex-Spitfire pilot called Ted Novak. Because of a heart condition, he had lost his licence, but was very much a back seat driver, and I think he would have flown through the eye of a needle if he could have got away with it!

It was a pleasant change from sea and rigs, and was almost like having one's own helicopter, for once we had delivered Charles to wherever he wanted, we could do virtually as we pleased. It was great fun, therefore, to arrive at Witherley Lodge one morning, park the chopper in the field behind the orchard, and have lunch with my doting parents!

The flying was not all fun, however, and at times we were asked to do tasks that were bordering on the dangerous – always a problem in this type of operation. I remember one specific flight when I had to take two of Charlie's friends down to their holiday cottage on Exmoor. For various reasons the flight was delayed, and we eventually arrived crossing the Bristol Channel in the dark. The last 10 miles were spent creeping up the moor following a road with the landing light until we were almost in low cloud. I decided at that point to land in a field by some houses and ask our passengers to make their own way to their house!

Although, at that time, there was no commercial helicopter instrument rating, I decided to use my naval experience, and made a vertical take-off straight up into the cloud, coming out on top at 3000' and diverting to Swansea airport to refuel. My Danish girlfriend, who had come along for the ride, was most impressed (or possibly totally terrified) and we had a lovely moonlit flight back to Cosgrove.

On another occasion, Tony and I had to pick up a couple with their two dogs from their farm nearby and fly them to Cranfield Airfield, where one of the jets was to fly them up to Scotland to join CMH for a shooting weekend. It was a horrible day, very windy with torrential rain.

We arrived near the farmhouse to find the only suitable landing site was a ploughed field. We loaded the passengers, dogs, luggage and guns into the back and managed to pull the skids out of sticky mud into a hover. Because of the high wind and the heavy weight, the only direction I could fly was towards an 11kw power line. These are the smallish lines one sees around the countryside, usually supported by twin wooden poles.

At the last minute, I decided that there might not be enough available power to fly over the cables, so I hover taxied instead under the wires. All was going fine until, thinking I was clear, I rotated a little too early and touched the main rotors. There was a bit of a blue flash and a pair of very panicky pilots. We landed a little further down the field and shut down the engines to investigate.

It was obvious that although the damage to two of the four blades was minimal, we could not be sure of stresses that may have occurred in the main gearbox – the helicopter could not fly – and so started one of the worst 24 hours of my life. It was pouring with rain, the dogs started shitting in the helicopter, the passengers had to get to the airport, and I had to apologise to my boss for breaking his lovely helicopter.

Somehow or other, we achieved all of that, without too much collateral damage; only to find the next morning that the nearby river had flooded and a £2 million pound flying machine was sitting in three feet of water! When the field dried out, we then had to tow the poor little chopper across three fields and four ditches to the nearest road, where it could be put on a lorry, to go back to the maintenance base at Blackpool for a complete overhaul.

This was at the end of September, and we did not get G-BAFD back until the beginning of November. By this stage, the Mackenzie-Hill empire was beginning to crumble; all the fixed-wing aircraft were sold, and even poor Tony Dando was made redundant; surprising considering my earlier faux-pas!

I continued to fly Charles around and about for the rest of the month, but eventually the pressure to fly in dangerous conditions became too much and I resigned. Of course, I should have just stayed on for another fortnight, when the company went into receivership, and collected some redundancy – but I was never too good at that sort of forward planning.

So it was back home to Witherley, and a chance to have Toby up from Devon for a time as Sally had now come back to settle in Topsham near Exeter.

How to eat humble pie and other stories

I had now been flying helicopters for nearly eleven years. This would have been an ideal opportunity to cross over and retrain as a fixed-wing pilot and join a major airline.

Instead, I decided to swallow my pride and return to Bristow Helicopters for another spell of rig flying. This time it was to Aberdeen, the Sikorsky S58T and back to the grey, cold and windy North Sea.

The great British oil exploration and production saga was growing in momentum. Aberdeen was a hive of activity, somewhat like the "Wild West" must have been like during the gold rush.

By late 1975, I had bought my first property, a top floor flat in Queens Road; a rather prestigious address in the city and very central for the pubs and night life that abounded all around.

I was now a Supervisory Captain, in charge of the 58T fleet of four helicopters. It was definitely not as glamorous as it sounds. The aircraft were rather ancient and were given the more mundane tasks at the base. One of these was an offshore operation based on the Forties oil field.

Four huge production platforms were being constructed, and our task was to be a glorified shuttle bus, taking about 200 workers onto the platform each morning and bringing them back every evening. At 12 a time, that was around 40 trips a day – sometimes when the accommodation barge was nearby acting like a flying elevator – it was hard and boring work!

In 1976, I was asked to do leave relief in Trinidad for three months. It was great to be back there, although life on the island was far tenser, primarily due to the Black Power movement throughout the Caribbean. Still, it was much better than droning around the North Sea, and after my work finished I took the opportunity of going back up through the islands; first to Barbados and then Antigua.

Here, whilst staying in English Harbour, I met a young Canadian guy, who was skippering a 50' yacht. We got on well and he offered me a berth up to the Virgin Islands where I was planning to meet a friend from Aberdeen. We had a great sail up there, stopping at St Barts and Saba.

In Tortola I spent a week with Colette, who was working in the marina, and who introduced me to the local social life. I also met a Swiss couple who were sailing their boat into the Pacific. They, too, were looking for crew, and offered a trip all the way to Australia. it was very tempting and I so nearly went off with them. The next year I realised what an opportunity had been missed.

Grumbles, trouble and strife

However it was then back to Aberdeen, and before long I was involved in a power struggle between a majority of the pilots and the Company.

Alan Bristow had been one of the first helicopter pilots in the Royal Navy. On leaving, he founded Air Whaling, invented a helicopter launched harpoon gun, and then started in oil rig support operations with a single helicopter in the Gulf. He was a tough and bombastic character and ran his company in that manner. So a group of his pilots wanting to join a trade union was very much like a red rag to a bull!

Before long, in April 1977, a small incident triggered a much larger dispute; and suddenly there we were, outside the airport base, manning a strike picket line. As a management pilot, I really shouldn't have been there; but, as a person with a conscience, I felt that I couldn't let down my chums. It was, as can be imagined, a fairly divisive situation; for aircrew, who share considerable danger at times and who depend on each other's professionalism and skill, were being torn between their loyalties to each other and to their employer.

After twelve weeks of stalemate and with the company just managing to keep a few of the aircraft flying, the Labour Government stepped in and arranged both a High Court enquiry and a transfer of all the 54 striking pilots to British Airways Helicopters.

It was, eventually, a face saving exercise to ensure that the vital oil and gas supply from the offshore oilfields was maintained and to placate both sides. As one of the four in the organising committee, I attended the Judicial hearing in Glasgow, and gave evidence face to face across the table from Mr Bristow. It was an interesting experience, to say the least, and thus brought the curtain down on that portion of my aviation life.

To Beccles and a new beginning

My earlier experiences of East Anglia were based on a stay at Great Yarmouth in winter, which must be one of the gloomiest places for a holiday imaginable. To be posted therefore to Ellough Airfield, near Beccles, not very far away, didn't seem the dream ticket for me.

But, I soon discovered that this small market town and the surrounding countryside were quite different. It was really very lovely, and the crews at the base were all immensely friendly. Being employed by British Airways was so different. The Captains were treated like gentlemen, and both the salary, and the benefits of staff travel in a major airline were so much better than I had imagined.

To start with I was put up in a local hotel down by the river in Beccles but before long, I needed to find my own accommodation, and Claire Woodage, the Manager's secretary at the base, suggested that I rent a room from her parents who lived next door to the hotel. They were all very kind and I really started to enjoy myself in this quiet backwater, away from the hustle and bustle of Aberdeen.

The work was also fairly easy. Offshore up to about 60 miles from the coast were about 16 gas production platforms, grouped in four areas. Our biggest task was to support the Britannia floating oil rig, which was drilling exploration wells up to 170 miles out in the middle of the North Sea. This could be quite exciting in the winter when weather conditions were sometimes rather marginal, and we had to avoid frequent snow showers, always with one eye on the fuel gauges!

Events of a slightly different type of excitement where beginning to happen elsewhere. Claire invited Bill Sutton and I, together with another couple to a supper party one evening. She was expecting a girl friend to join the five of us, but this lady was working as a cook at a local pub and came around rather later.

A very attractive, dark haired girl eventually arrived and was introduced as Widge Harkness. [50] In conversation, I mentioned that I had known a John Harkness whilst working in Pembrokeshire the previous year; in fact I had taken over a cottage he had been renting. It was such a co-incidence that this was her elder brother. She made a huge impression on me, and I was determined to meet her again.

Shortly afterwards, Claire mentioned that her sister, Sue, was getting married. The fiancée was selling his little cottage in a small village nearby, and would I be interested. Melrose was a sweet little house, set in about $\frac{1}{4}$ an acre with views across the marshes towards Beccles. I had just sold my flat in Aberdeen, and this seemed a great place to move to. Before long I was ensconced and my mother, Mishie, had even arranged a companion for me, a lovely cross Springer and Collie dog called Bess.

I discovered that a bachelor with an amiable dog is an excellent combination for drawing out the best in women; and so I seemed to spend more time having lunch at the "Loaves and Fishes" pub and chatting to the enchanting Widge. Frequently I saw her slim figure skipping around the town, usually in a yellow sailing smock. I started to plan my transits so that we would meet, and towards the end of the year, plucked up courage to ask her to the BAH Christmas dance.

It was a wonderful evening and, as I later discovered, she seemed to be very lucky, for she won the first prize in the raffle, an enormous turkey. After that all went rather quiet and I began to suspect that I might be the turkey, for there appeared to be another suitor! One evening I went on my own to see a film at a cinema in Lowestoft. By the strangest coincidence, there, just two rows in front, were my heart's desire and a man!! It was a rather odd situation, and spurred me on to an even greater determination to get to know her better. Before too long I had seen off my rival, and begun to meet all her family and relations around Beccles; not least, Annabel, her seven year old daughter from her first marriage.

---

[50] *Properly named as Philippa, but known as Widge because she was born prematurely, a surviving twin, and so small her father said she looked like a little Widgeon (duck)!*

The broken pieces of my rather turbulent recent life were beginning to settle down into a much more stable pattern, and Widge and Anny seemed just perfect to join Toby and I in a new family. So, on July 29th 1978, we were married in Lowestoft Registry Office on a very hot and sweltering day. Our marriage was blessed at Beccles Church amongst what seemed to be an enormous number of strangers, and we had a fantastic reception at her cousin, Ralph Montague's farm at Ringsfield.

Being new to a major airline, I had consulted my best man, Neil Charleton, on how to arrange a concession flight to our honeymoon destination, Mauritius. No problem – if I did this and that, I would be guaranteed a firm booking on the next day. So off we drove to Heathrow in a horrible rain storm, parked the car in a staff hangar, and proceeded to join the queue at staff check-in.

There seemed to be quite a lot of people there, and after a while, I found out that most of them were hoping to go on the same flight! After another wait, an announcement was made that the flight had been over-booked anyway – and our romantic bubble was well and truly burst! Such hopes and aspirations when you are young! With heavy hearts we retraced our steps to the car, phoned my sister, Ginger, and descended on her to spend the second night of our honeymoon – in London.

Eventually, the next day, we managed to arrange a week's holiday in Las Palmas, in a hotel full of highly organised Germans (all the pool loungers were bagged by breakfast-time), but love conquered all, and we had a great time with lots of laughs. Twenty years later, I made up for that awful lapse as we flew off to Mauritius for another honeymoon!

Moving up the Market

On Anny's ninth birthday, Bill Harkness and I went over to a little village a few miles south of Norwich to have a look at a house I had seen advertised for sale.

The Mere House was an absolute beauty. It sat across a mere[51] from the small road that bisected Seething and was incredibly picturesque. It had been built probably three or four hundred years earlier, but the front had been rebuilt in Georgian times. When Widge and I had a look around later that week, we were totally enchanted and felt that this would be the perfect home for us.

---

[51] Meres were created when clay was dug out for building wattle and daub walls for the local houses. This particular one had perhaps a diameter of 150 yards.

However, there was one huge problem – the property was to be auctioned. We had no idea what sort of price it would fetch, and we, ourselves, had only a limited amount of capital to invest. If we really stretched ourselves, £50,000 would be our top limit; it seemed a huge sum in 1979. So off we went to a hotel in Norwich, sat nervously anticipating the start of the auction. I remained silent until the bidding reached £45,000, and then bid just three times and amazingly The Mere House was ours. To this day, it has always remained my most favourite home and was blessed with a wonderful sense of goodwill and serenity.

New arrivals

Setting up in our new house seemed to spur Widge on to all sorts of creativity, including getting pregnant; for the following May, Katy arrived; to be followed just over a year later by a rather premature James. He was absolutely tiny, but once we got him home, he seemed to shake off his rather shaky start to life and soon became a vocal and energetic little boy. Toby and Anny had settled down really well together and bringing up the babies created a marvellously close knit family.

My incipient "do it yourself" skills were honed to the full at Mere House, and before long I was converting the attics, creating and redesigning the two bathrooms and helping my two friendly builders create a new dining room, outside utility and garaging. We also created another garden and installed a patio and brick barbeque. Life was very good and we had a incredible time in our lovely home.

.. and more new arrivals

At work, the two S58T helicopters were coming to the end of their working lives with BAH. The Company was beginning to grow as the oil industry expanded, and we now needed faster and more reliable aircraft. As the Chief Pilot, I was ideally placed to take charge of the introduction of the new Sikorsky 76 helicopter. So in October 1979, I flew out to Stratford, Connecticut, to accept our first aircraft.

This was my first trip to the States, and I was slightly overawed by the prospect of finding my way from JFK airport up to the factory. I had been informed that a room was booked in the local Hilton hotel, but when I arrived, having been driven there with other travellers in an enormous stretch limo, I found that no booking had been made and no rooms were available in any of the city hotels due to a large convention!

Feeling very tired and getting very frustrated, the doorman offered to fix me up with a room in a suburban motel. Eventually I arrived to be offered an extremely sleazy room, which looked more like a hooker's passion playground. All my worst fears seemed to be realised. I walked out of that situation very promptly, and consequently found myself in a MacDonald's restaurant. 5000 miles from home, very tired and very fed up and with just one contact phone number.

Luckily I managed to get hold of a Sikorsky executive, and told him I would be returning back to the UK unless proper accommodation was sorted out pronto. Eventually a decent small hotel was found and I enjoyed a few days in New England in the late fall before finishing a week's conversion course down in Florida.

The Spirit, as it was initially called, was a superb helicopter. It was sleek and very fast and I was hugely proud to be the first English pilot to fly it. In May, the first of the four aircraft arrived at Southampton Docks, and my Training Captain, John Millward, and I flew it up to Gatwick to show the bosses what a brilliant helicopter they had bought!

Unfortunately it didn't look quite so glamorous in early October, when, after John and I had been completing night landings trials on the Forties field, a main gearbox warning sounded. We had no alternative but to land and shutdown on the Forties Charlie platform to await an engineering check.

Later that night, I was awakened by the platform supervisor and told that very high winds had broken the tie-down gear holding the helicopter to the deck and that it had blown over!! Our lovely G-BZAC was a rather forlorn £3 million heap. The worst problem was that this particular platform was the point from which all the oil was piped ashore; the nearest crane was out of action, and unless the helideck was cleared by 10 am in the morning, oil production might have to stop. The alternative was to push the wreckage into the sea. Luckily they managed to get the only other crane at maximum stretch to hoist it clear and eventually AC was shipped back to Gatwick for a rebuild. I remember that when it returned to service, it always flew with a slight twist to the right!

In February 1980, I was back in America; this time in Conroe, just north of Houston, Texas, to accept our next S76; this one with a full Sperry auto-pilot to enable single pilot instrument flying. Eventually we had all four Spirits flying in and out of Beccles and Aberdeen. It was a super helicopter to fly, although there had been a number of unexplained accidents including a dreadful crash near Aberdeen, when one of my old Bristow friends was killed. The problem was eventually traced to a design fault in the main rotor blade attachment; a fundamental and disastrous technical fault, and certainly gave me and my fellow pilots a considerable feeling of unease.

Despite the rather erratic introduction of the Spirit into service, I seemed to have earned the trust of my superiors for in January 1982, I was given the task of introducing the next new helicopter. This was to be the Westland 30, a commercialised version of the Lynx which had been in military service for a number of years. My training Captain, Les Rose, and I stayed in a smart hotel near Yeovil and we were joined by a technical instructor, John Chicken.

I soon discovered that these two guys were the biggest inebriates I had ever known. Within a couple of days, they had drunk the hotel bar dry and then took me out on a run ashore around Sherborne where we became rather enamoured of a local beer called Tanglefoot. After about 15 pints in a few pubs, we got back and despite their protestations, I went off, very wobbly, to bed. I'd just got to sleep when the phone rang; the Hotel Manager told me that Captain Huggett, our boss from Gatwick had just checked in and needed to see me urgently.

I had been expecting a visit as we had become very concerned about the poor payloads the new helicopter could carry – not as many passengers as we had been led to understand. so, I threw on my clothes, and went down to reception. The Manager said Don had just gone to his room to freshen up, and would meet me at the bar.

Les and John were still propping up the bar and looking extremely merry – "have another pint", they said – "Don is just coming". So, reluctantly, I settled into yet another pint as the minutes dragged by. After half an hour, a rather old penny started to drop – this was a scam – the bastards.

The worst of that evening was the next day. Apart from a monumental hangover, and a huge effort to stay awake in the morning technical school, we had scheduled a test flight for the afternoon. This was to show how the Westland 30 behaved at maximum altitude. It was a brilliantly clear day, no cloud at all as we climbed up to 10,000 feet. It was only the second time I had ever been so high in a helicopter, but never before with so much alcohol coursing through my body! When Colin Hague, the test pilot, started doing maximum bank turns of 60° or so, I thought my head was going to spin off. It was utterly horrible, and my only satisfaction was looking back into the cabin and seeing an even greener Les Rose!

Showing the flag

As the Technical Pilot on the new type, it was my job to liaise with the manufacturer, particularly with regard to demonstrating the helicopter to all sorts of interested people in many locations. We flew it all over the UK and in May took part in the Hannover International Air Display.

This was great fun, and it was fantastic to be with so many experienced test pilots at the daily briefings. Don Huggett, our Gatwick

Manager, had been scheduled to come over and speak at a symposium at the prestigious technical forum on the performance of the Westland 30 and our operational requirements in the North Sea. At the last minute, I was told that he was unavailable and that I would have to make the address. So without any notes, I bull-shitted my way through 30 minutes before an audience of 150 technical pilots and engineers from around the world in the huge Town Hall!! My reward for that period of purgatory was a very handsome calfskin attaché case, which I still have today.

In September, we demonstrated the aircraft at the Farnborough Air Show, which included a lot of shuttle flights down to Battersea Heliport by the river Thames. In November, we were off again, this time around Scandinavia, where we did demos in Stockholm, Copenhagen and Oslo.

1982 became the high point of my flying career, for towards the end of the year, rumours began to circulate that British Airways, in the middle of a complete company re-organisation, were going to sell the Helicopter division[52].

Going backwards ... on my head

In order to encourage staff to leave, a very generous severance package was on offer. I had now been flying for nearly twenty years. I had been incredibly lucky in the postings and jobs I had been given, and had also managed to survive in body and soul, when quite a few of my mates had passed by. The future with a new employer and doing the same old offshore flying looked rather bleak, so I decided the time had come for a career change, and on 15th March 1983, made my last ever flight having accumulated just over 5000 hours as a pilot.

With a young family, it was going to be a difficult decision; should I perhaps try and join an airline, or get involved in the new technology of computers. In the end, I decided to take on a really challenging and thought-provoking job – I went back to the family business – hat making!!

My father had died in January 1980, and my Uncle John Stafford, who was the Chairman, was well over retirement age. His son, Michael, was eighteen years older than me, and the only other Director, Peter Herrmann, who looked after the felt-making department, was due to retire soon as well. It seemed an opportunity to get involved at the higher levels in the Company within a short time and, perhaps, to bring a little more energy to a rather old and staid industry.

---

[52] *Soon afterwards the company was sold to Robert Maxwell, an extremely colourful and ruthless newspaper "tycoon". In fact, he was a total rogue and plundered the remaining employees pension fund.*

My mother, Mishie, had now moved out of the family home to be with my elder sister, Jenny, and so Witherley Lodge was on the market as well, which would provide a large and commodious house for the family.

It was not, I have to admit, a hugely inspiring decision; and almost as soon as I arrived back in that Midlands backwater among those rather dour and strange Atherstone folk, I realised I might have made a monumental mistake!

Getting ahead ... with a hat

My biggest problem was just the different pace of life and attitudes of all the 110 employees we then had at Wilson & Stafford Ltd. It was all so slow and, frankly, so boring, after all the thrills of my flying life. Within six weeks, I had written my resignation letter, but for some strange and forgotten reason, I never did give it to Michael. Instead, somehow or other I slowly became involved; learnt more and more about hat making and all its history, technicalities, and personalities and gradually became more and more drawn in to this very traditional industry.

By September 1983, I was made a Director, and started to spread my managerial "wings". Of course, I had to absorb a huge amount of information on all of the aspects that drive a business. Starting from the technical production processes to marketing, sales and personnel management; it was a fairly daunting initiation, particularly in an old established firm, where trade practices seemed always to have been committed to memory, sometimes passed down to the next generation; but quite frequently forgotten over the years. For myself, used to the rigorous aviation disciplines that required standardisation, checks and balances, the hat industry was more than just a revelation – it was something of a nightmare.

The factory had been manufacturing since 1871[53], and buildings had been added, seemingly indiscriminately, ever since. The result was a veritable rabbit warren, with the production snaking up and down two or three floors and over the 48,000 square feet in an apparent miasma of confusion.

Tracking orders was a monumental task and the whole setup was creaking on the verge of collapse. My first task, in the administration area, was to introduce office computers; to move payment of wages from a weekly cash distribution to a four-weekly bank payment, and to investigate a computerised production control system. Shock and horror swept the factory! Their comfortable little world was being rocked by

---

[53] *For more on the history of Wilson & Stafford Ltd, refer to the Appendix*

the new guy, and all the old horror stories of how this and that business had gone to the wall due to over ambitious and new fangled ideas were regurgitated and flung hither and thither!

The new broom

In a play produced in Atherstone in 2001 depicting the rise and fall of the Hat Industry, I was obliquely referred to as "the New Broom". It was meant to be derogatory as some of the more socialist elements in our workforce felt that my policies had created the conditions that saw the demise of Wilson & Stafford Limited.

Writing now some ten years after the event, I am really quite proud of what was achieved by the Company during the 16 years I was involved. There were, understandably, mistakes made; decisions regretted; hindsight is a great judge. However, a small and rather colourless business became within ten years, one of the larger headwear manufacturers in the world, selling to major high street stores such as Debenhams, BHS and Laura Ashley, producing a wide range of hats from toppers to cloth caps and panamas to seductive millinery.

We took over the other two Atherstone manufacturers; Austen Aspden in 1986 and Vero & Everitt in 1988, and at one point employed 250 people. Our production became computerised, our machinery was improved and our work force was happy.

In the early nineties we were producing a quarter of a million hats a year, our turnover had increased from £800,000 to £2.8 million and our profit stream was healthy. I would have loved to have shown my predesessors, and particularly my father around our bustling factory; I was very proud of our achievements.

Meanwhile ....

Whilst I was moving hat factories and people around Atherstone, the family were rapidly growing up. Toby, aged 16 when we settled at Witherley Lodge, went to the local High School, before deciding to move away from home, ending up in Ipswich, where he discovered the delights of sky-diving, girlfriends and working as an assistant engineer in a bacon factory.

Anny, who was a day girl at All Hallows School near Bungay, stayed on as a boarder for the next four years, before moving on to a finishing college near Loughborough.

Katy and Jamie started their journeys through education, beginning at the little church school in Witherley and then moving on to the Dixie Grammar in Market Bosworth. From there, they went for a final year boarding at Loughborough Technical College, where most of their time seemed to have been spent partying.

Katy ended her education at the Chilterns University based at High Wycombe, where she gained a BSc in criminal psychology. Widge, after a while, joined me at the factory and became involved in millinery design as well as learning pottery at Nuneaton Technical College.

By 1988, we felt that Witherley Lodge was just too big for us, and decided to build our dream house in the orchard. We had originally determined on a timber Scandinavian design, which would have been really good. Unfortunately, trying to save money, I got involved with a local architect and builder, who translated the original design into brick.

Although eventually a very nice house when it was completed, it took ages to build. During the six months of construction, the national housing market went rapidly from boom to bust!! We were left in February 1989 with two houses, one we couldn't sell, but felt we should live in to keep it looking good, and a brand new house next door, for which we had a massive bridging loan to finance! Not entirely the best position to be in.

At long last, in early 1991, we found a buyer for the old house. John and Jo Connell became very good friends, and Widge discovered the delights of pottery through Jo's expertise. It was very sad to part company with my old home, but we knew that it would be in good hands.

In time, John and Jo made some lovely improvements all over the house, and even converted the old stables to a pottery workshop. In 2007, they, in turn, moved on, and so now Witherley Lodge has become a distant memory.

Animal magic ...

My old dog, Bess, came with us to the Midlands, as did Olly, Anny's marmalade cat, which she had been given for her 9th birthday. Sadly, after two years, dear Bess had to be put down; and Judy Wathes, who had given her to me originally, introduced us to another waif, a cross Dalmatian and, we think, Labrador, who we named Bitzi. She was rather wild to start with, and we found she had a passionate hatred of red motor bikes! But she was actually a great, if somewhat unpredictable dog, who loved to run and run.

In 1995, whilst visiting Mishie, I found myself returning home with an extra passenger – a small brown and white Springer Spaniel puppy who we called Buster. The rest of the family, returning from a visit to Beccles, were delighted to find the new addition scampering around The Orchard, our new house, in to which we had moved in January.

Buster was to become the grandfather of two of our present dogs, Bobby and Braveheart, sons of Bruno and Bella. A little later, my arm was severely twisted to allow Katy, who was then 13, to have a horse; and so a five year old gelding, Benson, joined the four legged gang.

the end of an era.

In March 1999, reflecting a fairly hefty loss for the previous year and a poor sales forecast for the year to come; Lloyds Bank decided to cancel our overdraft facility. Unable to raise enough finance in the few days allowed, we had little choice but to accept their recommendation to go into administration.

We had been struggling to restructure the business for the previous four years; imported hats and hoods, mainly from China, had been flooding the UK market for some time, and naturally had had an adverse effect on our markets.

Our first step, in 1995, had been to close down the felt making department. In itself, this was a sad decision to take as we were the last piece felt manufacturer in the country. Ever the pragmatist, I decided to source the hoods from China, and after several visits found a suitable partner.

At this factory, located some 100 miles south of Beijing, we were given the full VIP treatment, including the most enormous banquets, often running to over 20 courses. Despite our fondness for oriental food, Widge and I became extremely nervous when the subject of eating came into the conversation.

For a while, we held our own, but when the Chinese began to ship container loads of hats over to Europe, we knew that the days of large scale manufacturing for us were over. In the same year, I managed to cultivate an introduction to an American shipping millionaire who had a particular fondness for hats.

He had already bought the doyen of the men's headwear trade, Christy & Co of Stockport; but was very interested in our management style and much improved production lines. At our final meeting, he offered to buy the company for a little over £1 million. Whilst that offer was quite good, and would have impressed my shareholders, I felt that it was very likely the production would be quickly moved overseas[54], our employees would be made redundant, and my own position would be degraded in some respects. So, I refused, deciding instead to continue merger discussions with a similar sized company based in Luton called Olney Headwear.

I was to discover the truth about the old proverb "a bird in the hand is worth two in the bush"! Shortly afterwards Olney's, out of the

---

[54] *After our refusal, he purchased a smaller cap manufacturer, and eventually, within a year moved, all the production to Sri Lanka*

blue, had a family boardroom coup, and the new Chairman immediately called off our merger plans. And my fears of redundancies for the workforce were fully realised just over three years later, when receivers were appointed and the business was closed down almost immediately.

To stand in front of so many old and familiar faces on that April morning and tell them that after 128 years Wilson and Stafford was to be no more, was a hugely bitter and emotional experience – without doubt, the hardest and cruellest words I have ever had to utter. For the shareholders, there was no consolation at all; their shares[55] were worthless and I was the rascal who had fouled the family nest egg! Three generations of Stafford's glared down at me as I left the factory for the last time.

And the beginning of another chapter

In the autumn of the previous year, we had already decided that we would be moving away from Atherstone. My parents had lived in Witherley for nearly fifty years without any incidents, yet over a period of eight years we had been burgled three times.

With that insecurity plus the huge increases in road traffic along the Watling Street, and the general degradation of life in the Midlands, it was becoming more and more of a strain on all of us in the family. For me, there were the added stresses of managing an ailing business, and my nerves were being stretched far more than was healthy. This had, of course, a big impact on Widge and the children, and it was becoming obvious that if we were going to properly enjoy life, we needed to turn a new page.

In 1998, Anny suggested we have a short holiday with her at Croyde in North Devon. I had never been to that area before, and we both loved its wonderful beaches and the rugged coastline along the Bristol Channel. One morning we were having a cursory look at some wooden chalets for sale near the beach, and a couple stopped us, asking if we were interested in their cottage which they had just decided to put on the market. We drove back to the Midlands that Saturday, the proud owners of The Wendy House, and so our love affair with beautiful Devon was born.

That October, we sold The Orchard, and rented a small cottage in Witherley, whilst we investigated houses for sale all over Devon. In the end, we found the perfect spot was only five miles from Croyde.

---

[55] *Although I had the largest number of shares – 10,000 of which I had bought myself.*

It was Buttercombe Barton, a large stone built former farm house with the date 1086[56] over the front door. The name alone evokes peace and tranquillity, and its position in a small valley a mile from the village of West Down, and with its own ¼ mile drive and 18 acres of meadow and gorse could only enhance our determination to settle there. It also had an adjoining holiday cottage plus an empty barn ripe for conversion, so that an additional income was guaranteed.

So although the events in early April 1999 were traumatic, we had largely decided our future path, and fortunately for me, there was little time to dwell over the factory's fate or to bemoan too much on the circumstances that had caused it.

On 28th June 1999, a day after my 56th birthday, we packed our bags and drove down to the south west to begin a new and exciting life in deepest Devon.

Living the Good Life

As I write this, our tenth anniversary at Buttercombe is looming. This is the longest we have been in one house, and this one house and it's surroundings has been our love and joy for a decade. Looking back to the chaos and humiliation of 1999, it is almost impossible to imagine that life for us down here could have been so blessed.

We have made many friends and done a host of things and enjoyed almost every single day. We have kept pigs and sheep and hens and created gardens and built a cottage and a hut. We have learnt to put up gateposts in squirming mud; retrieve lost sheep, take a large sow for a walk on the hillside and endure floods amidst wet Devon winters. It has been such fun.

---

[56] *Despite extensive research, I have never substantiated this date. I think it refers to the year the Domeday Book was written, and is probably a whimsy of the previous owner, Mark Loosemore. A house has undoubtedly been standing on this site from around that time, or earlier, but the present house has been extensively remodelled since Georgian times.*

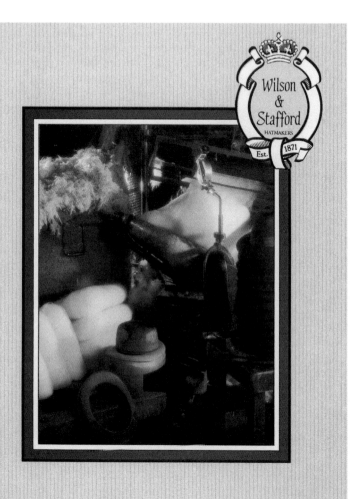

Wilson
&
Stafford
HATMAKERS
Est. 1871

A TRADITION IN FINE HEADWEAR SINCE 1871

When I was very young, perhaps in 1948, a visit to "the factory" was a real adventure. We travelled the mile or so up into Atherstone from our house, fronting the old Watling Street at Witherley. At that time, I think we had a Morris 8; rather small, with brown leather seats, finger indicators and very slow!! With Mummy could have been my older sister, Angie, and more probably my younger sibling, Virginia, always known as Ginger, who would then have been three and a bit.

Atherstone was built on and around the old Roman road, and the main thoroughfare was, rather obviously, called Long Street. Halfway along past the Regal Cinema and next to the Red Lion Inn, we turned left into Coleshill Road, leading south; there, just over the humpback bridge, next to the Coventry canal was, what seemed to me, the most enormous building – the hatmaking works premises of Wilson & Stafford.

In 1936, seven years before I entered the world, my Grandfather, Will Stafford, had presided over the opening of the New Building; a three storey, flat roofed, brick and glass structure rising up directly from the canal. This provided some 50,000 square feet of production space, and coupled with the much older areas, parts of which went back two or three hundred years, occupied a large triangular area surrounded by small back streets and rows of terraced houses.

We may have parked over the road from the factory, where the firm owned another piece of land, which included a building housing the carpenters who made the crates that delivered our hats all over the old British Empire[57]. However, it was more likely that Mum would drive down Richmond Road to the rear entrance, where Alan Tingay reigned over the hand operated petrol pump.

The factory was dominated by an enormous brick chimney, which took the smoke away from two huge Lancashire coal-fired steam boilers. These had been installed by 1913 when this photograph was taken. Steam was the essential ingredient in so many of the hatting operations during the production cycle, and throughout the factory plumes of steam could be seen issuing from windows and vents. This visual experience was accompanied by the constant rumble of machinery and the unforgettable smell of damp wool that pervaded the air. The epicentre of this Dante's inferno was in the hardening[58], bumping[59] and planking[60] shops on the ground floor of the new building. Here, in the foggy half-light, figures could be seen moving piles of felt hoods in various stages of manufacture, whilst a battery of what, to a small boy, seemed like amazon-sized women battered the felt hoods into submission.

My father, Ernest Stafford, was the Managing Director, and looked after the Ladies Hatting department from his office on the top floor of the "New Building". His elder cousin, Mr John, was the Chairman, and supervised the Men's hat department from a small and ancient office at the front of the factory overlooking Coleshill Road. Next door to this was the General Office, where four or five ladies dealt with the administration, typing, orders and wages under the supervision of Alf Moores, who was large, genial and ever cheerful.

Mr John's son, Michael, was also involved in the Men's hat production, and was often found behind enormous piles of boxes in the packing room; whilst the Feltmaking department was managed by

---

[57] *I remember boxes and crates going to Australia, Canada, Kenya, Rhodesia, South Africa, Trinidad, Barbados, Malaya, India, Ceylon, Burma, Hong Kong and many other countries.*

[58] *Hardening was the first felting operation, where the form was placed, with a triangular cloth inside, between two alternating plates. The plates were covered in a rough canvas fabric and steam injected through the bottom plate. Under dynamic pressure, the wool fibres would shrink and be interlocked, so starting to form a strong unwoven fabric. The tip was similarly felted on an adjoining cone*

[59] *Bumping machines were the same as fulling machines; used since medieval times for shrinking woven cloth. A pair of huge oak hammers alternatively pounded the planked hoods in an oak-lined chest within a cast iron frame.*

[60] *Planking involved a machine fitted with grooved wooden rollers in which the hood was rotated vigorously.*

Peter Herrmann, whose own family had been in the hatting trade in Germany. Helped by my Grandfather, he had come to England in 1937 and so had been one of those lucky people to have escaped Hitler's Jewish persecution. Sadly, many of his family died in the holocaust.

Whilst the newer canal-side building had large, open and airy spaces; the old buildings were a rabbit warren of stairs and small rooms; all of which seemed to be populated by a different family of people. There were the leurers, the blockers, the proofers, the tip-stretchers, the steamers, the rounders, the trimmers and the packers. We young children would all be greeted by "oohs" and "ahhs" – and a warmth and friendliness which could only have come from a happy and contented business; despite the very basic working conditions and low pay rates.

If we were very good, we would be taken to the canteen where Mrs Morris would give us a delicious treat to relieve the monotony of food rationing. I loved the engineers shop, where the Shiltons, Harry, George and Joe would be beavering away at some reluctant machine in their oil smelling blue overalls; or along to the dyeshop where Ernie Davis would preside over his chemical empire of magical colours and steaming dye vats.

In comparison to the other offices, my father's was almost luxurious. Here would be the ever bustling Dolly Myering, who had been the mainstay of the department during the war. Situated on the top floor of the canal-side building, one could look out on the market town of Athertone and northwards over the rolling Leicestershire countryside, to where the Stafford family had lived in the eighteenth and nineteenth century.

The beginning

My great grandfather, Richard Stafford, had come from a farming family in the small village of Ratcliffe Culey, two miles north of the town. He had trained as an accountant and found his first employment with Hall and Phillips, who then occupied Joseph Wildays "model" Hat Factory in Station Street. In 1872, he had formed a partnership with William Wilson, the felt manager, who was well acquainted with the skills of felt-making, since both his father and mother had come from local hatting families. Together they had purchased the hat business of William and Katherine Simmonds, who had employed about 20 people between them during the previous decade located on Coleshill Road and by the south side of the Coventry Canal.

This area of the canal basin and wharves, previously known as Pinchbeck's Mill, had been connected with the making of hats and the transportation of raw materials such as wool and coal since its inception in 1771.

Initially a partnership, the business soon established itself as a leading company in the town, employing more than 300 people by the 1880's. In 1890, the firm became a limited liability company and continued to expand both in the home and export markets.

... and into the 20th Century

When Richard Stafford died in 1917, he was an extremely respected figure in the town and left a considerable estate[61]. By then the firm, together with its great competitor, Vero & Everitt, were the two largest hat and felt-making companies in Atherstone, and the foundations had been laid for more growth as the Great War was ending.

He was succeeded by his eldest son, Henry Angrave, and William Denis, my grandfather, who was to become the driving force for the business after Henry died through ill heath in 1923.

Mr Will or "WD", as he was known, despite his kindly and rather avuncular looks, was a bit of a tartar. He had a habit of being by the workers entrance by 7 o'clock in the morning when work started and any late comers were then turned away; tough treatment in the hard days following the war. He also had the reputation of refusing to see any trade suppliers who did not wear a hat!!

I hardly remember him as I was only three and a half when he died in 1946, but he certainly brought the factory through the heady days of the twenties and thirties, and the confusion and hardship of the Second World War. In that period, part of the factory was commandeered to produce parachutes and other war necessities, and many of the employees were away fighting, including both my father and his brother, Uncle Richard. Henry Angrave's son, John, however, being too old for active service, remained as Managing Director, together with Peter Herrmann.

Sadly, just after the war ended, Uncle Dick died, and grand-father shortly afterwards in December 1946. My father, who had always entertained the idea of an engineering career, was rather forced by these events to return to the business soon after the war ended to manage the Ladies hat-making department; a situation I think he always rather regretted.

I was to join the firm shortly after my 17th birthday for after eight years of boarding school it seemed just the job for me and infinitely preferable than a further four years education at University.

---

[61] *He was a member of the Atherstone Board of Guardians and the old Rural Sanitary Authority and became Chairman of the Parish Council. He was very interested in the Atherstone Cricket Club for over fifty years. He left an estate worth £21,819, which would be over £1 million today.*

My father, ever the innovator, thought it best that I start learning the ropes by commencing my hatting career at the finished product in the packing room; and then working my way backwards. Unfortunately, whether due to labour demands or perhaps my youthful awkwardness, I was rather forgotten there for some time, before being suddenly shovelled into the dyeing department.

Here I spent the rest of my eighteen months of employment; trying to learn the mystery and secrets of felt dyeing, and desperately trying to avoid the unsubtle ministrations of some of the more aggressive females in the hardening shop[62]; whilst perhaps being a little too friendly with the prettier girls elsewhere.

Much to my father's huge chagrin, I decided to leave my chosen career after this short time to work in a lovely pub in Long Street – The Three Tuns; the work being less onerous and better paid than the rather miserable £6 per week I earned for a fifty hour week at the factory. After a further spell selling cars for a local garage, I eventually saw the light and knuckled down to the challenge of joining the Royal Navy. It would be 21 years before I returned to the firm as an older and wiser man.

The management in 1960
– from left – Bill Parkin, Peter Herrmann, Gertie Cotton, Ralph Thomas, Ernie Davis, Alf Moores, Ben Dingley, Annie Shilton, Harry Smith, George Warner, Tony Stafford (dogsbody) Ivy Dingley, Michael Stafford (back), Harry Shilton, Dolly Myring, John Stafford (Chairman), Ernest Stafford (Managing Director)

---

[62] *It was, I understood, the practice to initiate apprentices by smothering their tender nether parts with grease normally used for lubricating the bumpers – or perhaps they were just having a laugh at my expense!!*

A big decision

Gradually as the century progressed, the economics of the new Elizabethan age, with greater wealth, car ownership and modern fashion saw the gradual decline of hat-wearing. The fortunes of the company also declined in parallel. The formality of business became a distant memory; men no longer walked or cycled the streets under a flat cap; only the old ladies still wore a "Wilstaff" felt hat; school outfits became far more casual and baseball caps and beanies became the preferred headwear.

My father died in 1980 and by then the management had devolved upon Michael Stafford, John's son and Peter Herrmann. Over the years, many other hatmakers around the country had been forced into closure so it is to their credit that our company with two others in Atherstone remained in business. However in an effort to contain overhead costs, a considerable part of the factory had been let to other unrelated businesses; employees now numbered under 100, sales were declining, and decisions on the continuity of management were looming fast.

In 1983, after twenty years flying around the world, I also had to make an important career decision. As a shareholder, and knowing a little of their concerns, I decided to write to Michael to see if a management opening was available.

It must have been an opportune time, for by April I had swapped helicopters for hatmaking machines, and settled into the still bewildering world of wool, blocks and fashion.

... getting ahead

By 1986, we had negotiated a takeover of Austin Aspden, and moved their production from Long Street to Coleshill Road. The main attraction of this deal was a major broadening of our product range, so that we now manufactured fabric hats and caps, straws and military headwear as well as felt hats and caps. We also acquired a number of experienced workers to add to our now increasing workforce. In 1988, we also merged with Vero & Everitt to take over their hat and felt making interests as well. We decided to lease their more modern factory in Station Street for our hat production, and merged all of the felt-making production in the better part of Coleshill Road. We were now one of the largest hat manufacturers in the United Kingdom employing some 230 people.

Since I had come back as Managing Director, we had also embarked on major improvements to our office information systems. Archaic production control was superseded by computer based order processing; employees were no longer paid weekly in cash, but "persuaded" to transfer to a four weekly cashless[63] system; and new or better machinery was sourced and installed.

Although these changes brought us back into the modern world, I sadly discovered that over the many years since 1871 that some of the best felt-making techniques had been forgotten and so we seemed at times to be re-inventing ourselves. I think Great Grandpa Richard might have been rather scathing about our quality, but I like to think that all three of my previous family generations would have been very impressed at our production and profit figures.

Whilst the hatting industry was but a shadow of its' former self, we still had occasional bursts of great activity – the Princess Diana phenomenon, when her hat-style became a fashion sensation; the countryside hat favoured by the Cotswold set, and the felt-blocked cap, which we sold in many thousands, especially to Italy where it was a vital accessory, worn backwards, for scooter riders!

By now, we were supplying very large hat orders to BHS, Laura Ashley, C&A, Debenhams and other large store chains, as well as the Ministry of Defence to whom we supplied WREN officer hats, Ghurkha slouch hats, cold weather hats for the Bosnian war, and many thousands of desert fabric hats for the 1st Gulf War.

After three years operating on two sites, we found this to be very onerous from a production point of view and expensive in overhead costs; so the old factory was renovated with better offices and showrooms and the production process streamlined to improve efficiency. The costs of this move were managed to some extent by our much higher turnover and profits ...

.... and going down

But like so many industries, there is always a constant shifting between fortune and failure. As part of the ever-changing fashion scene, we were even more susceptible to these pressures. The whole hat industry since the 1950's had shrunk enormously; once prosperous firms had collapsed; rumours abounded of this firm or that in trouble, and competition was fiercer than ever. However, from 1994, imports from the Far East began to grow significantly; particularly in wool felt hoods and the cheaper hat products.

After a large loss in 1995, we decided with great reluctance that the felt-making department was no longer cost effective and that we should investigate the possibility of buying hoods from China.

---

[63] *No mean feat where employees were as set in the old ways as sure as their surroundings!*

In 1997, we entered an agreement to be sole distributor for hoods in the UK for a major Chinese manufacturer, and consequently our felt production closed in early 1998.

In the meantime, we had been supplying both Bhs and Debenhams with large orders. Initially, this was extremely encouraging, but as we progressed from season to season, their price demands became more and more unrealistic, so that by late 1997, we had decided we would be unable to realise anything near our required margins, and therefore these sales were lost.

Our export sales, traditionally at some 35 - 40% of turnover were also being hit by the high value of sterling. As a third blow, felt hat sales became very depressed, partly due to the variable weather during that year and to ever increasing competition from baseball caps and very cheap ladies fabric pull-on casual hats.

At the beginning of 1999, with an overdraft approaching £500,000, our bankers, Lloyds, carried out an audit on the business and decided in April to call in their loan. At that point, with no alternative funding available and with huge regret we had no option but to put the Company into receivership.

By the end of that month, after 127 years the factory became silent. The wonderful machinery was sold to a Russian company for just £100,000. The buildings were sold to a local developer for the same amount, and have steadily deteriorated over the last 13 years. There has been talk of converting to flats or demolition but so far nothing has been done.

EPILOGUE

A couple of years after the factory closed, I travelled up to Atherstone from our new home in North Devon in response to an invitation to see a new play produced in the town; written with the help of some of our old employees. I believe it was called "The New Broom".

It illustrated the story of an American researching his roots in the town, and discovering that the old hat factory where his grandfather had once worked had been recently closed. The essence of the plot was that a new Managing Director had arrived at the Company, changed the old ways of working, spent more money on "improvements" than was wise, and, of course, as a consequence the business had failed. It was quite an experience in that room to feel the spotlight shining bright on me as the obvious villain of the piece.

Now after the years have mellowed the shock, disappointment, and even heartbreak of that time, I can reflect more sanguinely on the history of our company from its beginnings to its end.

Family businesses are renowned for their ups and downs, their family squabbles; reputations built up by the first two generations, to be destroyed by the third or fourth.

However, in Wilson & Stafford, I really believe that most of the people who worked there over the generations, from the top to the bottom, had a real and genuine affection for the business. Despite the working conditions, and in an often hard and unpleasant environment, they were nearly always cheerful, gave willingly of their labour, and wanted the firm to do well. They were all proud to be part of "the hatting".

I always felt that way myself. From my earliest recollections as a small child to the day I had to tell the employees the end had come, I had wanted the Company to be the best, and for me to do my best for both it and those who worked in Britannia Works. But the end could have been different ... at least for myself and my reputation!

In 1995, we received an offer to sell the business for something over £1 million. The deal would have been completed, but for the fact that I knew the production would, after a short while, be moved overseas to a cheaper labour market; the factory would be closed in Atherstone, and our employees made redundant. So, by unanimous agreement, the Directors decided to refuse the offer.

Had we known what was to transpire four years later, I'm sure we all would have seized that opportunity. But perhaps as the Chairman, I was not really that good a businessman; not hard enough to make the tougher decisions; carrying too much emotion and the sense of my place in a long established family business. .... and .... perhaps, in those circumstances, we, the Directors, might have been accused of selling the business out; feathering our own   nests; of letting the employees down .....

As a final thought, I wrote this poem a few years ago – my personal tribute to "the Hatting".

Ode to a Hat Factory

The undertakers came to the factory today
they peered and they prodded, dressed all in grey
and the bustle and laughter drifted away

We told the workers the business had closed
because our bankers had suffered cold toes
and the look in their faces reflected our woes

from the boss to the cleaner, all herded away
given their cards, not wanted this way
and the hats in the showroom make the saddest display

Hardening, planking, blocking and trim
shops where they steamed and they sweated in
now standing empty, so cold and so dim

Machinery sits silent, it's work is now done
Ending the years of thunder and drum
for us it worked wonders; to strangers just scum

The rumours were right, they knew all along
the Company was going to be sold for a song
so why had it all gone so horribly wrong?

Fashions had changed – times had moved on
Hats were so longer an essential creation
They no longer inspired a sense of occasion

Sacrificed to volume, those skills we had built
from generations of hatters whose sweat had been spilt
in rickety rooms as they laboured in felt

The ghosts of the past no longer appeared
Frightened by failure they so often had feared
In all those one hundred and twenty seven years

all that experience built over time
a rich tapestry, embroidered , sublime
and now like a toy unravelled in grime

so remember the hatters, those characters bold
who gave of themselves, a heritage old
until that sad day the factory was sold

The front of the factory circa 1919

The original gas powered Tangye engine which drove all the machinery throughout the factory by a system of drive shafts and belts.
I remember it as a young boy – no safety guards to speak of and it all looked incredibly dangerous.

We used a tremendous amount of steam to heat water for dyeing the hoods and in all sorts of ways for felting, blocking and shaping the hats. These two enormous Lancashire coal-fired boilers provided all that from the turn of the century until they were scrapped in 1984

This photo from 1913 shows some of the forming machines we used to start the felt-making process
.A fine web of wool was wound on to the forming cone as it rotated until the required thickness and weight was achieved when it was cut by shears to form two "forms".
Note the drive shaft and belting which powered the machines

The Hardening shop in the 1960's – "whilst a battery of what, to a small boy, seemed like amazon-sized women battered the felt hoods into submission"

Grace Ambrose proofing the hoods – probably 1970's

Finishing a hat using sandpaper.
Sometimes we also used sharkskin to give a slightly longer finish

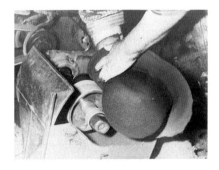

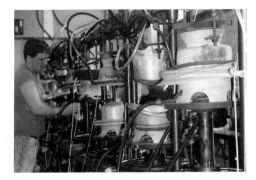

a line of gas heated blocks - mainly used for millinery

the traditional shaping method using a wooden block and frame to make a topper. The block comes apart to remove from the crown

APPENDIX

Included below are various documents, references and information the Felt and Hat Making Industry. There is also a very interesting video made at the factory in 1997 which shows the felt-making department before closure – the end of this process in the United Kingdom.

http://www.friendsofatherstone.org.uk/hattingvideo.htm

Extract from the 1841 census in Atherstone
Old House Yard, 1, John Hall, 60, Hatter
Sarah Hall, 60,
William Beadman, 40, Day Labourer, Not in county,
Old House Yard, 1, William Simonds, 60, Hatter
Mary Simonds, 55

Atherstone Hat Making Companies in 1899 (Atherstone Street Directory)
Austin. R.W. Owen Street
Denham & Hargrave (became Austin Aspden Ltd – bought by W&S in 1986)
Eliott, F.J. Kitchen's Buildings, Long Street
Epplestone, E.S., Stevenson's Yard, Long Street
Hall & Phillips (moved to Nuneaton in
Hattons, Vinraces Row, Long Street
Thomas Townsend & Co, South Street
Wilson & Stafford, Coleshill Road
Vero & Everitt Ltd, Vero's Yard, Station Street

From 1914 Whitakers Red Book
HAT AND CAP MANUFACTURERS
mostly based around Manchester – those still operating in 1983 in bold type
(See also Straw Goods)
Bainbridge Brothers (Leeds), Battersby and Co, Richard Burley
Butt, Vosper and Knight (Tweed Caps), Carruthers Brothers
Christy and Co, S. Cooksey and Co, Gaunt and Hudson
Hall and Phillips in Nuneaton – formerly in Station Street, Atherstone
Henry Heath, James Higinbotham and Sons, Victor Jay and Co
T. and W. Lees, Lincoln, Bennett and Co, J. Moores and Sons
Moores, Birkby and Brown, Morgan and Taylor, James E. Ogden and Sons
James Robinson and Sons, Thomas Townend and Co (having moved to Stockport from Atherstone), Wigston Hat and Cap Co,
Wilson and Stafford, J. Woodrow and Sons , J. Woolfenden and Co

The Art of Feltmaking had entered England in the reign of Elizabeth I and was originally centred on Southwark in London. It spread north to Cheshire and Lancashire in the early 17th Century and was active in Chester in 1629. It reached Coventry by 1636; introduced by Edward Owen, where it replaced the woollen cap- making industry which was so important to that city during the 15th and 16th centuries.

Felt hat making was first recorded in the Atherstone area in 1658 and became the main source of occupation for the working people of the town until the 1920's, along with the local coal mining activities.

Although London and Northern hatters produced mainly fur-felt derived from beaver and angora rabbit pelts; Atherstone appeared to have developed as a centre for wool felt production. This was almost certainly due to its central position in the country where herds of sheep were traditionally driven from area to area.

Hatting flourished here during the 18th century. The Atherstone " Cordier " (a term possibly derived from the French town of Courdebec, which was also a centre for wool felt manufacture); was a favourite in the days of the slave trade; mainly due to a statute of George III which required all plantation owners to provide suitable head wear for their slaves.

With the demise of the slave trade, the early 19th century brought other business opportunities. During the Napoleonic war, Atherstone was supplying the army with Shako helmets and other forms of headwear. Peace, and the growth of England's industrial might, saw great changes for the Atherstone hatters. Until the late 1850's, feltmaking had been a hand-crafted process. The American Civil War brought dramatic advances in clothing manufacture which also included hatting. Such developments introduced machinery, not only to the northern hatters of both continents, but also to Atherstone.

The History of Hatting in Atherstone[64]

The earliest felt caps were knitted in the round from yarn, and then felted in troughs of fuller's earth. This capping trade was carried on in Coventry from medieval times. Hatting spread to Atherstone in the 17th century.

In 1672, Samuel Bracebridge, a "Haberdasher of Hats" (i.e. a merchant) was supplying materials to cottage feltmakers. Atherstone was well suited to the trade because of a plentiful supply of water and fuel.

In 1696 Joseph Hatton, feltmaker, wrote his will:

"In the Workhouse 2 poore old kettles & 3 Sorry Basons and Hattblocks & other old lumber"

Valued at 9 shillings and 4 pence.

Before factories were built, felt hats were made in small workshops in the yards behind houses in the town. Using a 'feltmakers bow', the feltmaker would produce a bundle of wool, termed a "batt". The batt was separated into two equal parts of a roughly triangular shape and pressed gently between a hurdle and a piece of leather. It was then taken to the "bason", an iron plate over a small hearth where the feltmaker pressed it, sprinkled water over it, and worked the wool gently so that it began to felt.

The two triangles were then folded together into a cone shape with a piece of cotton cloth inside to prevent the sides felting together. Using steam and pressure the men worked the felt form until it shrank to almost a third of its size. Next the felt hood was dried, stiffened and blocked.

Trimming was done by the women of the family, often outside on sunny days as most of the workers lived in the 'yards' where there was very little room indoors. By the 1790s a number of hatters workshops had become established in Atherstone and many families were moving into the town to work in the trade. A shortage of land was forcing the intensive development of the yards behind the houses. Narrow dwellings lined the yard and a hatters' workshop often stood at the far end.

Census-taking started in 1851 and this and subsequent records show that half the houses in Bingham's Row had a hatter as the main breadwinner. Many had 2 or more occupants earning a living by hatting.

---

[64] from friends of Atherstone website - www.friendsofatherstone.org.uk

The Entrepreneurs

From the 16th to the early 19th century, hatting in Atherstone was a cottage industry, organised by five generations of the Bracebridge family. Cottage feltmakers collected wool from the Bracebridges, took it home and made it into hoods during the time they had to spare between tending their crops and their stock.

By the 1780s the Bracebridges had sold out to one of the most prosperous of the cottage feltmakers, John Wilday, who had taken an apprenticeship in London, and was also a banker. By this time specialised premises were developing. John Wilday's son, Joseph, set up the first purpose-built hatting factory in Atherstone. After Joseph Wilday died in 1852, the premises were leased by Hall and Phillips.

Charles Vero's family had been hatters in Atherstone since 1786. His brother-in-law, James Everitt, was the son of a tallow chandler with premises where the Somerfield supermarket is today. The two men formed a partnership on the eve of a voyage to Australia in 1851, where they set up a hat shop in Melbourne.

In 1855 Charles Vero returned and rented from W.S. Dugdale, a premises in the "South Backway" in Atherstone. Over the next fifty years, Vero & Everitt's factory expanded.

Machinery was introduced in the mid-nineteenth century, and Vero & Everitt filed several patents for improvements in the processes. Hats were exported all over the world from the factories built in the middle of the town.

Hall & Phillips relocated to Nuneaton. However, by the early years of the 20th Century there were a number of substantial hat factories in Atherstone:

Denham & Hargrave, F.J. Elliott & Co., Thomas Townend & Co.

W.A. Hatton Ltd, Vero & Everitt Ltd, Wilson & Stafford Ltd

In 1986 only three remained:

Austin Aspden Ltd, Vero & Everitt Ltd, Wilson & Stafford Ltd.

Feltmaking in Atherstone ceased in March 1999, when Wilson & Stafford went into liquidation. Vero & Everitt Ltd continued to manufacture a small number of uniform hats in the town until the site was sold to ALDI for a supermarket..

An information leaflet I produced in 1986

About Wilson & Stafford Limited

Our Company was founded by William Wilson and Richard Stafford in 1871. Mr Wilson's family had long been involved in the hat wholesale business in Birmingham and he had been working with another firm of local hat manufacturers. Mr Stafford was the son of a local farmer who had decided to enter the rapidly expanding hat industry. Together they bought the disused flour mill on Coleshill Road in Atherstone.

Atherstone in those days was a major centre for the wool felt hat industry. Twelve factories in the town employed in excess of 3,000 people manufacturing hats of every type which were exported all over the world. Those were heady days for the hat industry. New technology and machinery had revolutionised the hat making processes, enabling mass production of felts and hats for the first time. Everybody; man, woman and child; wore hats.

After the Second World War, with the growing popularity of cars and public transport, there was a rapid decline in hat wearing generally. It saw the demise of many other felt and hat making companies in this country and abroad.

However, Wilson & Stafford is still going strongly as a family business, now into the fourth generation.

Today, we employ 195 people making what is probably still the largest range of headwear in Europe. Whilst we rely on the traditional ways of making and creating hats, we continue to invest in new technology to ensure that British hat making survives into the 21st Century.

Our range of hats embraces ladies millinery in wool felt, polyester, straw and velvet; to men's bowlers and toppers. From fezzes (still exported to Africa) and fedoras to combat and uniform hats and peaked caps for the Services. We make fabric hats and caps from Harris Tweed and waxed cotton; felt caps and trilbies to hats made especially for theatre and films.

We pride ourselves on our traditional heritage that started back in 1871. We still occupy parts of the original factory although we have modernised and enlarged our production facilities. However, the quality of our hat making still reflects the standards established in those early days.

William Wilson was well acquainted with the skills of felt-making since both his father and mother had come from local hatting families. Richard Stafford was a member of a Leicestershire farming family, but having trained as an accountant, had entered the trade in a management capacity in the 1860's.

The last member of the Wilson family to be active in the management of the Company was Charles Wilson who died in 1912. Since the turn of the century, members of the Stafford family have continued to oversee the business; the present incumbent being Tony Stafford as Chairman and Managing Director.

Wilson and Stafford absorbed the feltmaking interests of Austin Aspden Ltd (formerly Denham & Hargreaves) and Vero & Everitt Ltd during the 1980's. It remains as the last standard bearer of the wool felt making tradition not only in Atherstone but throughout the United Kingdom.

Another leaflet produced in 1993

The Atherstone Hatters

and their place in headwear fashion down the ages.

A survey of the evolution of the Hat in relationship to the Atherstone Feltmakers

From Tudor times in Southwark, London, felt hatmaking spread through the provinces reaching Coventry by 1636 and probably Atherstone shortly afterwards.

Fur felt hats of Elizabethan and early Stuart times where exclusively for the rich man, and were known as 'Beaver Gallants'. The cost of a single beaver hat would pay a labourers wages for a year.

Charles I had beaver skins brought from his new colonies in Canada to make the 'Chimney Pot' hat he wore at his trial in Westminister Hall.

The interregnum saw a hat made of firm wool felt with a high tapered crown known as a 'Sugar Loaf', which was favoured by Puritans and Quakers. Their founder, George Fox, (who was born in the village of Fenny Drayton, a mile to the south east of Atherstone), was so attached to his hat, he refused to remove it when examined by magistrates as a recusant. Samuel Butler, a feltmaker of Hartshill, another local village with a strong Quaker community, must have made many 'Sugar Loaf ' hats during the 1650's and 60's.

Wilson & Stafford still produce a replica for the Sealed Knot Society from our largest hood size

The Restoration retained the shape but not the plainness of former times. The late Stuarts embellished their hats with silver buckles and bands of gold and silken thread.

By the close of the 17th Century, crowns had become round and low and the cottage workshops of Atherstone's hatters were multiplying fast. In the early 1800's the large floppy brim was beginning to be 'cocked' or folded up at the front of the crown. This new style was called the 'Billy Cock' – attributed to bullies who roamed the expanding towns. Atherstone preferred, however, to give the credit to Joseph Willday who monopolised the local felt-making trade at that time. By 1730, the brims were cocked into three equal sides to create the tricorne- the eternal image of the 18th Century.

The tricorne is still a specialty of W&S, and is supplied to the female Officers in the Royal Navy (formerly the WRNS), and to various other civilian services.

During the 18th Century, the local hatters were doing good business with the slave trade as the plantation owners had been forced into providing hats for their slaves by a statute of George III. A cheap simple wool-felt known as a 'Cordy was produced to satisfy the demand.

By 1780, the 'Bicorne' was replacing the Tricorne especially with the Military. The brims were cocked front and back or at each side. They were heavily braided and bound at the edges and sometimes Cockaided.

Regency England saw crown heights rise once again, tops flatten and brims shrink. The result was a style popular with Dandies such as Beau Brummel.

Early 1800's saw a further raising of crown heights and the straightening of sides. The 'Top Hat' was born, a style adopted by all classes of the population up to the 1850's. The Wellington, a top hat designed by the Iron Duke, had a reverse tapered flat crown and a curled brim. A shortened version was popular with the artisan class symbolized by the character of Mr Pickwick of Dickensian tales.

Silk plush toppers with high straight sides were initially stretched over a wool felt base, but later a stiffened calico for lightness was used. In the town, silk hatters William Miller and Richard Hatton were trading very successfully. The exaggerated 'Stove Pipe' top hat with a 7" crown of polished beaver or rabbit fur brings early photographic images of I.K.Brunell and Abraham Lincoln to mind.

W&S continues the top hat tradition today with a range of wool-felt toppers for the Wedding and Dress Hire trade

When Joseph Wilday died in 1852, Atherstone saw the end of a hatting dynasty that had dominated the local scene for more than a century. In the 1860's, two young hatters, William Wilson and Richard Stafford were learning their craft with the local firm who succeeded the Wildays. In 1871 they formed a partnership and established themselves on the site from which we still operate alongside the Coventry canal.

James Lock, the oldest established London hatter still in existence and established in 1676, was approached in 1850 by a Norfolk landowner named William Coke, and asked to produce a hat suitable for his gamekeepers to wear, as theirs were continually being blown or knocked off in the woods, and being damaged before they were worn out. William Bowler of Southwark, a hatter who supplied Locks came up with a low round crown, highly stiffened, which Coke tested and approved by standing on the crown.

Another age, that of the 'bowler hat' had been created. A variety known as the 'Derby' was a favourite in the American market. In 1889, another well known London hatter, Herbert Johnson, was offered the patronage of the Prince of Wales, and created an indented version, known as a "Homburg" after the Prince saw the style on a visit to Germany. This hat remained popular well into the 1940's, and was a favourite of both Winston Churchill and Franklin Roosevelt. Even as late as 1950, Atherstone hatters were presenting their version to Sir Anthony Eden, the Conservative leader on a visit to the town.

The 1920's. 30's and 40's were the heyday of the trilby, and local hatmakers took their share of the market. Demobilisation in 1945 brought the last great boom in the hatting industry. The new freedoms of dress in the late 50's and 60's and the increasing popularity of the car heralded a general decline in hat-wearing and many well-known firms faded away.

Early 19th Century Atherstone did not neglect ladies hat fashion, although it was dwarfed by the huge Millinery industry in Luton, seventy miles to the south east. Straw bonnets of Chip, and 'leghorn' (derived from the old name for the Italian town of Livorno, long regarded as the finest straw plait in the world) were being produced by Mary Gregory on the premise of her hat shop and at four other sites in the town.

The Company still makes a wide range of straw hats using genuine Panama's, sisals, and xians.

Military hats such as the 'Shako' had been supplied since Waterloo and felt or cork helmets covered with cotton drill were made in great numbers in the town from the time of the Zulu wars to Britain's retreat from India. A tighter crown type covered with wool serge was made until the 1920's and is still popular with the English police forces.

The service or frame cap has replaced the helmet as the main uniform hat. Essentially this is made of woollen melton or worsted cloth with a stiffened side crown and a black patent leather peak.

This is now the latest addition to our headwear range, alongside an amazing variety of shapes in felt, straw, tweed and soft fabric to satisfy the varied tastes of today's customer.

The Craftsmanship and expertise of 300 years of the Atherstone Hatter has been concentrated and matured in the hands of Wilson and Stafford - the last wool feltmaker in the United Kingdom.

an extract from the The Worshipful Company of Feltmakers of London

Brief History of the Feltmakers

The first known reference to Feltmakers as a distinct craft association is in London in 1180, although it is not known how long this lasted. In 1269 the Cappers became officially established. Hurers made shaggy and bristly caps at that time and in 1311 the Hatters are found carrying out an examination of hats at the Guildhall. Faced with the need to combat imports, obey the new Act of 1488 restricting sales prices and enforce the ordinances controlling the trade, the Hurers and the Cappers amalgamated with the Hatters and then merged with the powerful Haberdashers in 1502. Many of the feltmakers were already members of the Haberdashers and, as the Haberdashers controlled the retail outlets and the raw materials, this unification of the hatting trade, no doubt, seemed a sensible step. The Feltmakers were the only group to survive in name and became synonymous with hatters and is today the Livery Company of the hatters.

In the middle of the 16th century discord developed between the Feltmakers and the Haberdashers from whom they were forced to buy their raw material of wool in 'sacks unseen'. This led to much unrest and in 1583 they petitioned Queen Elizabeth I for their own Charter. This step was vigorously opposed by the Haberdashers. It was not until 1604, when King James 1 came to the throne and needed funds, that the Feltmakers were granted a Charter of Incorporation – the first of eight granted at that time – in the name of 'Master, Wardens and Commonaltie of the Art or Mysterie of Feltmakers of London'. The cost was £500 and it was claimed there were 'seven thousand persons of the said trade'. In 1667, King Charles II granted an expanded 'Charter of Confirmation' extending the powers of the Feltmakers. This was confirmed again by King George III in an Inspeximus Charter in 1772.

In 1733 the Company was granted Livery by the Court of Aldermen. The Company is number 63 in order of precedence.

One of the historical stories of the Feltmakers refers to Queen Elizabeth I who, on her journey to Tilbury in 1588 (at the time of the destruction of the Spanish Armada), was passing down Holborn Hill when she was met by a cheering crowd of well-dressed men wearing polished beaver hats; these were the hatters from Blackfriars and Southwark, the then centre of the hatting industry in London. It is reported that Her Majesty, much struck by their lusty demonstration of loyalty as well as their appearance, enquired who "these gentlemen were?". On being told they were journeymen hatters, she replied "then such journeymen must be gentlemen". The description stayed and journeymen hatters were referred to as "the gentlemen" until well after the First World War.

In the period 1870-74, 11 famous politicians joined the Feltmakers. They included W H Smith, Cecil Raikes, Rowland Winn, Admiral Hay, the Earl of Iddesleigh and Sir Edwards Hicks Beach. Between them four had been Chancellor, two First Lord of the Admiralty, two President of the Board of Trade and two Foreign Secretary as well as being the holders of many other high offices.

The hatting trade flourished and the Company grew strongly in the early part of the 20th century. Between 1914 and 1918, 27 Mayors and ex-Mayors were elected. In 1927 there were 9 Knights on the Feltmakers' Court. However, during the second half of the 20th century, the trade declined to its present level. There are now some 170 Feltmakers and members are drawn from the higher ranks of many professions, businesses and trades as well as the hatting industry. The Feltmakers have produced two Lord Mayors, Sir Louis Newton in 1923 and Sir Hugh Wontner in 1973. A third, Sir Thomas White, Lord Mayor in 1876, transferred to the Vintners, as was the custom in those days, after serving as Sheriff.

A Day at A Hat Factory

The Penny Magazine, published monthly, contained an article in January 1841 on the manufacture of beaver Hats at Christy's Southwark factory. At this time some mechanisation had obviously been introduced.

Wool carding, fur cutting and blowing were done by machine, driven presumably by belt drive from a central steam-engine. However, all other processes were achieved by hand or manually operated tools - jobs which required considerable effort and skill. Not least was the total time spent on making a fine beaver top-hat - possibly 12-15 hours of continuous labour.

At that time the production process was as follows:-

The hat was made in two parts - the body and the covering.

The Body was made of a blend of wool and coarse fur.

The wool arrived as a shorn fleece, which was washed and dried before carding.

The various animal skins, beaver, musquash, neutria (now known as the coypou, which following the increasing scarcity of beaver pelts was imported in vast quantities - upwards of one million skins a year), hare and rabbit were also washed and the outer guard hairs removed by hand and discarded. The remaining fur was cut by machine from the skin and blown to remove the thicker hairs, which were used in the body, the fine fur reserved for the covering.

The constituents for the body were then weighed out (8 parts rabbit fur, 3 parts Saxony wool and 1 part llama, vicunia or "red"wool). 2

and 1/2 ounces, enough for one hat, was placed by the "bower" on the bench in his compartment.

The bow, made of ash, was suspended from the ceiling just above the bench. The catgut cord was then plucked with a piece of wood causing the cord to vibrate rapidly against the wool and fur. After a time, this created a very light, soft and perfectly mixed pile of material.

Once bowed, the material was divided into two portions. The first was pressed into a light wicker triangular frame, approximately 18" wide by 18" tall, and then covered with a piece of oil-cloth or leather called a "hardening-skin" and continually pressed with the hands backwards and forwards until a coherent fabric was made. The other half was made in the same way. These " batts" are then laid flat, and a piece of paper, smaller than the triangle was laid on top of the first part; the edges are turned over and then worked together with the second batt to form a hollow cone with the paper in between to stop the middle felting together. This felting process was achieved by folding into a damp cloth and working on the bench by hand.

After this initial felting, the conical "cap" was taken to a hatter's "kettle"; a central copper with a fire beneath, surrounded by a sloping octagonal planked arrangement. The planks were made of mahogany, with a lead covering at the water's edge. The caps were frequently dipped in the boiling and slightly acidulated water and then rolled, twisted and pressed with a wooden pin for about two hours until the felting had been completed and the cap had shrunk to about half of its former size.

After drying, the cap was water-proofed with a mixture of gum-lac, gum-sandrach, gum-mastic, resin, frankincense, copal, caoutchouc, spirits of wine and turpentine applied by brush with greater amounts being applied to the brim. The cap was then dried again to evaporate the spirit (incidentally, a very dangerous procedure which caused numerous explosions in hat factories at that time).

Scouring the cap with a weak alkali solution prepared the body for the next step which was the application of the covering of the fine beaver fur. This was made in a similar way to the original hardened cone, and was known as the "ruffing". It was laid over the body and patted down with a wet brush, with a little on the inside to form the under-brim. It was then wrapped in a woollen cloth, immersed frequently in the kettle and rolled on the plank for another two hours. This procedure forced the finer beaver fur into the body, and the nature of the fibre formed a permanent bond to it. In fact, in earlier times, the ruffing was often executed so well that the fine hairs penetrated completely through the body; so that when the outer surface of the hat became too well worn, it could be turned inside out and refinished. At this stage also, the cap was being turned into a hat by the working up of a brim.

The dyeing (invariably to black) was accomplished by continually immersing a rack containing up to 270 hats within a vat using a mixture of shredded logwood, water and metallic salts. This may have taken up to 8 hours to complete before the felt had been thoroughly dyed.

The hat was then blocked and the nap raised and leured before the final binding, leather and lining was added by the trimmers. At last, the hat was given a last brushing and the most fashionable brim set by the "shaper".

At this time, the article indicates that the hat factory of Messrs Christy employed 1,500 people at the two factories in Bermondsey Street, and that the combined annual sales value of the English Hat Industry was no less than three million pounds.

The Great British Hat Makers

During the late 19th and early 20th centuries, Britain (and specifically the North West) was the undisputed hat manufacturing capital of the world. In 1907 some 16,500,000 hats were made in the UK, a large number of which came from Denton and Stockport's 36 hat manufacturers.

This is an article I found recently. Apart from the advances in power generation, the processes of felt and hat manufacture had hardly changed.

MESSRS HALL AND PHILLIPS' HAT MANUFACTORIES, ATHERSTONE AND NUNEATON.

Extracted from an article in the Nuneaton Observer of Friday, August 29th, 1879

The good St Clements was making a long and weary pilgrimage. The way was rough and stony, and the Saint's feet were miserably sore, insomuch that his walk became a hobble, and he doubted if he could ever accomplish the weary miles that lay before him. In a moment of happy inspiration he noticed that tangles of wool had been caught from the backs of sheep on the thorny bushes of the waste. He gathered handfuls of the softest and finest, and with these made a downy padding in his boots for his bleeding and blistered feet, and was then able to resume his pilgrimage with greater comfort.

What has this to do with hats or hatters? The tradition is that when the Saint arrived at the end of his pilgrimage the soft wool padding with which he had lined his boots had become a firm and consistent fabric. The Saint had discovered the process of felting, and is regarded as the patron Saint of all felt hatmakers. Saint Clements' day is the hatters' holiday. Every hatters' apprentice then expects a present from his master, and in hat making towns like Atherstone the children go from door to door, singing a quaint rhyme, beginning, "Clements'ing, Clements'ing year by year, Apples and pears are very good cheer." This legend of Saint Clements is perhaps just as true as many another historical tradition. The history of the august Roman Empire begins with the story of two children suckled by a wolf. The history of felting begins with this legend of Saint Clements' sore feet.

Probably in the middle ages every village had its own working hatters, as it had its own tailor, and shoemaker, and glover, but it seems rather uncertain when the manufacture of hats on an extended scale for export to other districts and other countries was first introduced into Atherstone, which is its chief seat in Warwickshire.

Early in the last century a business of this kind was being carried on at Atherstone by one of the Bracebridge family, from whom it was purchased by one Joseph Willday. The business continued in the hands of succeeding generations of the Willdays for more than a hundred years, and in 1853 it was transferred by the representatives of the last Joseph Willday to Messrs. Hall and Phillips, by whom it is still conducted on the old premises at Atherstone, which are yet the property of a descendant of the Willdays, though extensive additions have been made to the works by the present firm. There are now several other hat manufacturers in Atherstone, but we select the works of Messrs. Hall and Phillips as representative of this branch of local industry.

The history of their business is the main story of the history of the Atherstone hat trade while in their extensive works not one branch only, but every department of the manufacture is carried on. The business carried on by the Willdays in the last century was extensive, the armies which fought our battles in America, India, and in the great war with France which ended at Waterloo, being largely supplied with hats from Willday's factory. As early as 1745, the year of Prince Charles Edward's daring but luckless attempt to recover his father's kingdom, the round hats made of soft rough felt then known as Atherstone Cocks, were not only sent all over the kingdom, but exported to the American plantations. The late Joseph Willday so increased the manufacture of these cheap felt hats, that they were named after him "Willdays Cocks," whence arose the well known term Billy-Cocks. The actual processes of manufacture were carried on in a very primitive form even down to the year 1862. Till that year the wool was carded by means of a bow with a catgut string, which the workman twanged near the heap of wool he wished to open out, the vibration of the string catching and opening the separate fibres. The felting was also performed entirely by hand.

In 1862 a strike occurred among the workmen. The immediate consequences were no doubt serious to employers and workmen, but this struggle hastened the introduction of the present system of manufacture by machinery which has led to so great a development of this industry. So extensively is machinery now utilized, that it requires four powerful engines (two at Nuneaton and two at Atherstone) to work the machinery used by Messrs. Hall and Phillips.

In 1868, the large premises at Atherstone proving yet too small for the ever increasing business, Messrs. Hall and Phillips removed a portion of their machinery to the Abbey Mills, Nuneaton, and it is there that the earlier processes of Body-making and Felting are carried on. The Abbey Mill is a large modern factory adjoining the walls and looking down upon the ruins of Nuneaton Abbey. To these mills, lands which were all unknown when the Abbey walls were reared, now send their unwrought produce. From Australia, New Zealand, or the Cape, come these huge tightly packed bales of clipped wool. Canadian rivers have been plundered to furnish these packages of Beaver fur; South America sends the fur of the Nutria; while from all parts of the United Kingdom the prolific rabbit and shy hare yield their furs also for manufacture into hats.

It will be best perhaps to follow first the processes employed in felting wool, the various furs being treated in a different manner. The wool being released from the bales which the shippers have packed in closest compass by hydraulic pressure, is first passed through a revolving frame of spikes, which bears the ugly but forcible name of a devil. By this machine the matted wool is broken up and loosened. From thence it goes to the washing machine, where it passes under a brass cylinder, into a large tank of hot water. It is passed along the tank by the action of rakes with long iron teeth till being sufficiently cleansed, the wool is fished out of the water by a set of forks worked automatically, and delivered on a higher level to a set of rollers by which it is wrung nearly dry and flung out at the further end of the machine.

The drying is completed by spreading out the wool on heated iron plates. It must pass through yet another machine to clear out the burrs or seeds which cling to the wool, and it is then ready for carding. It is only in one or two remote corners that old fashioned workmen hidden away in back yards still twang the ancient catgut bow. At the Abbey Mills the wool is carded by the same machinery as that which is used in carding cotton. Passing round a large cylinder covered with innumerable fine wire teeth, round which revolve a number of smaller rollers, similarly covered with wire, every fibre of the wool is opened, and it is delivered a fragile gauzy web. This web passes again through a smaller and finer carding machine, and as the filmy gauze is again delivered it is guided by the girl who attends the machine on to a revolving wooden block in the shape of a double cone, either cone being advanced alternately so that the gauze shall be laid evenly over each, excepting that for a given number of revolutions the wool is wound straight round the centre of the block - that is to say round the part nearest the base of each cone - greater strength and thickness being required there for he brims of the hats. An indicator affixed to the machine shows when the requisite thickness has been attained, and enables the work-woman to adjust the weight of wool to the mere fraction of an ounce. With a pair of scissors the work-woman then cuts the wool round the centre of the block and takes off from either end a hollow cone of wool, the "form" of a future hat which is now ready for the first process of felting called "hardening".

If a little carded wool be moistened and warmed by steam, or by breathing up it, and then chafed between the hands, it will be found that the fibres shrink and harden together. This illustrates the elementary process of hardening felt. Each soft downy cone is set on a metal shape through the perforated top of which ascends a jet of steam, and the vibratory pressure of something like a drum head hardens the "tip", or crown of the cone. The cone is next folded, a cloth being placed inside it, and laid on a table heated by steam, and having a vibratory or "jigging" motion A board, in shape, something like a large flat iron, and very heavily weighted, descends upon it, and the moist warm wool is subjected to the same "jigging" pressure from above and below. This is repeated, the hat body being differently folded each time, till it is sufficiently "hardened" in every part. The hat body being roughly felted, is sent into the warehouse for examination, for supposing any thin places to be discovered it is not yet too late to remedy them.

This ordeal passed, the next process is that of milling, which is effected in two ways, the object in each case being closely to shrink the felt and obtain that even clothlike surface which is one of the attributes of a good felt hat. In one of the departments of the Abbey Mills, this is effected by "Milling stocks", such as are used in milling West of England Cloth. Each hat body is rolled up singly and a number of them, perhaps fifty or sixty or a hundred dozen, are placed in layers in a receptacle above which hang suspended sets of huge wooden hammers. Hot water is poured over the hat bodies, and then the hammers descend alternately, dealing heavy blows on every part of the mass, steeping in the hot water beneath them, till not only is every hat body sufficiently "pleached" or shrunk, but the desired cloth-like surface is acquired. In another department the same result is obtained by different means; the hat body, rolled up in a cloth, is dipped in hot water and passed through sets of rollers having spiral bands which as it were grind it between them on its passage from end to end. There are in this department a large number of these most ingenious machines; the workman who feeds one machine, also receiving the bodies which are delivered from the next machine fed by his fellow opposite. Having been "knocked up" that is straightened, by hand, by a workman whose tool resembles a rolling pin, the hat body at present more like an extinguisher than a hat, is now ready to be dried and packed off to the Atherstone Works to be dyed, finished, and trimmed.

The manufacture of hat bodies from fur must be separately described. We have said that the principal furs used are those of the rabbit, the hare, the beaver, and the nutria. These furs are subdivided into many varieties and the same animal's coat is not all of the same quality, or suited for the same purpose. For instance, the fur of a rabbit consists firstly of two distinct divisions, the outer or grey coat, which consists of long coarse hairs, and the inner or fine coat next to the skin which is a short, fine, rich coloured fur, very delicate and smooth to the touch, so much so as often to be manipulated and passed off for sealskin. Even this fine fur known in the trade as "coney wool" has its own subdivisions, and is sorted out as "coney backs", "coney sides", "pate wool", "red neck" etc., these names indicating the parts of the animal, each of which furnishes a different quality. As many as 240,000 rabbit skins were used by Messrs. Hall and Phillips last year.

The first process of cutting and sorting the fur is carried on at the Atherstone works but can be most properly described here. The outer or grey coat, useless for felting, is first plucked from the skin by hand, a knife and the thumb effecting this with tolerable ease when the skin is in proper condition. A very ingenious machine is used for cutting the fine coat of "coney wool" from the skin. The skin is passed through finely grooved rollers and as it presents itself keen spiral plates fixed on a revolving cylinder cut off a strip of the skin about the size of a piece of twine. It is the "pelt", or skin itself, which is thus cut away in fine strips from the fur, the fur itself being returned by a back motion on to the table in front of the machine with hardly a hair disturbed, while the strips of the "pelt" fall below. The fur thus separated from the "pelt" is sorted out into bags as coney backs, coney sides, pate wool etc. The fleeces are "locked up", that is, slightly compressed together by hand as it were into a ball, and stowed carefully in paper bags for despatch to Nuneaton. At Nuneaton the fur is yet more accurately sorted by the "blowing machine".

The fur is delivered in at one end of what appears like a set of cupboards some 20 feet long. Three shelves traverse the whole length of the cupboard, and a current of air travels from the point where the machine is fed, backwards and forwards along the whole length of these shelves. By The finest and lightest fur travels the greatest distance, and is received in the furthest compartment. A middle quality is received in the central compartment while the coarsest and heaviest hairs reach no further than the first compartment. So unerring is the law of gravitation that it is found effectual in assorting "trifles light as hair."

The atmosphere is yet again used with still more wonderful results, in the next process. The fine short fur does not require carding like wool. The body of a fur hat is actually blown together, and that too by an arrangement whose simplicity makes it only the more marvellous. A cone of perforated zinc stands on a revolving table and the air underneath this cone is continuously exhausted by a fan. The exact weight of the fur to be used in the hat is delivered into the machine, in which another fan is revolving at a great speed, and the mouth of which is exactly opposite the metal cone. The one fan drives the fur like a cloud of fine dust onto the perforated cone; the other fan exhausting the air beneath, the fur clings to the revolving cone over which it is evenly distributed by the steady current of air. When this has been done wet flannel is wrapped round it, and the cone with its fur coating is lifted off the table and plunged in a pan of boiling water. After this hot bath the fur is removed from the cone, and is found to be already matted into a fabric.

What is known as "planking", or felting by hand, suits best the earlier processes of felting fur hat bodies. A circular stand or table sloping inwards, surrounds a well or copper containing boiling water. The workman rolls up the hat body as tightly and smoothly as possible on his table, and dips and works it in the boiling water. This is repeated continually, the fold being changed each time until the fibres have acquired the leathery consistency of felt.

The old fashioned white stuccoed building fronting the Long Street, at Atherstone, which was Willday's warehouse for over 100 years, would mislead a passer-by as to the magnitude of the business carried on by Messrs. Hall and Phillips. One must pass through the passage to the rear, and will there find a whole street of workshops and warerooms stretching through to South Street on either hand, and with intricate courts branching out to yet more shops. These Atherstone works have not been arranged on any regular plan, but their extent and their intricacy illustrates the growth of this ancient business. Block after block of buildings has been added on, where room could be obtained because room must be had, and although the heavier part of the work is now done at Nuneaton, there is yet no room to spare.

The firm make their own gas, and at one time these works supplied the town of Atherstone. They also make their own hat blocks, and the numerous packing cases they require for home and shipping orders. The bundles of conical pieces of felt which are sent over from the Nuneaton Works are not hats, but only hat bodies.

At Atherstone the felt bodies are first waterproofed or stiffened by dipping them in strong solutions of gums, and then steamed in an oven to drive the stiffening from the surface into the body of the felt. They are next spread to dry in the stoves, a set of rooms with perforated iron floors, in which the temperature is maintained at 150 to 180 degrees. On leaving the stoves the hat bodies are ready for dyeing.

It would be interesting, if space permitted, to describe how the huge piles of logwood are split up into small chips, and how the other dyes used are apportioned to produce the exact shades required by varying fashion. We can only stay to remark the capacity of the huge vats, some of which hold 600 or 700 gallons of liquid dye.

The future hat, when dyed and dried, is after all this labour, still only a brimless cone, the mere embryo of a hat, in form and appearance like a Dunce's cap. It must be fashioned into shape, the first process of which is blocking. When this is done by hand, the felt is softened by dipping it in hot water, and is stretched tightly over a wooden block of the required shape, while the brim is flattened out on the table on which the block is placed. A most ingenious machine effects this more quickly. It is as though a hundred metal fingers grasped the edge of the hat body, while a wooden block ascends and shapes the crown, and a circular rim descends from above, and simultaneously flattens out the brim. The hat body now begins to look like a hat, though the brim is flat and shapeless.

We next enter a workroom, and along the whole length of the tables on either hand are wooden hat blocks, or lathes, revolving at the rate of many hundred revolutions per minute. This is the finishing and lathing room. The hat is steamed, and while softened by the moisture and heat, the crown is more exactly fashioned to the required shape and size, and is then placed on one of these lathes. The youth who is working at it scours the surface of the revolving felt with sand-paper, to raise a fine nap, and with a velvet brush, aided by the swift lathe-like motion, smoothes this nap into uniform and glossy evenness.

In the manufacture of hard felt hats, not only is a stronger solution of gums used in the process of stiffening, but the hat is shaped under a high degree of hydraulic pressure. The hat body softened by heat is laid in a strong iron mould of the exact shape and size required. An India rubber bag filled with water descends and fills the crown of the hat. By means of powerful pumps water is compressed into this elastic bag till a pressure of from 300 to 600 lbs. per square inch is obtained.

The elastic bag, of course, yields easily and evenly. The more stubborn felt must also yield under this enormous pressure till it has taken the exact shape and size of the massive mould which holds it. We saw several of these massive iron moulds, which had burst under the pressure of a column of water forced into an elastic bag.

The crown of the hat is now properly fashioned, but the brim is still flat and shapeless. The shaping of the brim is one of the most delicate processes of the hatter's art and requires careful manipulation. The edge must be curled; the sides turned up; and at the back and front a slight downward inclination must be obtained. To obtain these results – to make the hat not only fit but seem to fit the head that wears it – the workman must have some measure of that artistic instinct which abhors abrupt angles and inharmonious curves. The shaping of the brim is therefore entreated to specially skilled workmen, by whom, the felt having been softened by heat, the brim is curled and fashioned to the required form by the application of heated irons and deft fingers.

The hat is now made, but the plainest hat requires to be trimmed. The edges must be bound; the crown must be lined; the leathern band must be stitched within the hat; and the silken band fixed round the crown. The lining itself generally bears some device, and this is printed on the premises. To accomplish the almost endless stitching, there are from forty to fifty sewing machines always at work in the trimming rooms, some of them ingeniously adapted for working two needles at once. With this large number of these delicate machines in constant use, we are not surprised to find that the constant attention of the skilled mechanic is required to keep them in repair. A vast number of hats are also given out to be trimmed by workpeople at their own homes, thus affording home employment to the wives and daughters of many of the employees of the firm.

The bodies or foundations of silk cloth covered hats which are also largely manufactured by Messrs. Hall & Phillips, are made of thin light calico, dipped in shellac and other gums in solution, and shaped on frames of the required size and form. The bodies thus fashioned are varnished and the outer covering of silk or cloth is stretched on to this light foundation and in the case of the ordinary silk hat, manipulated with heated irons and brushes, till not only does it adhere to the foundation, but a perfectly smooth and highly finished surface has been obtained. These hats are now often lined with a thin layer of cork, so finely cut as to be no thicker than a

sheet of this newspaper. The light porous qualities of cork have led to its adoption for the actual body or foundation of many hats, more especially for police and army helmets. Last year Messrs. Hall & Phillips executed one contract for 10,000 of these cork helmets for the use of English troops in hot climates.

Notwithstanding the length of this article we have only described the manufacture of such hats as are now most commonly in demand. To get some idea of the extent and variety of the multitudinous forms of headgear which have left this Atherstone hat manufactory for all parts of the world, we must look into the stock and warerooms. Here we are shewn not only every size and shape of hard and soft felt and silk hats worn by sober common place Englishmen, but also the policeman's helmet, the felted bottoms for Lancers' hats, the venerable threecornered hat worn by Chelsea Pensioners, the colliers' sump, the light military helmet for tropical service, the broad brimmed soft shepherd's hat, the pauper's hat, the Slave's hat, such as was formerly exported for the use of negroes on American and West Indian plantations, though now chiefly in demand for some of the native tribes of South Africa, the light coloured high crowned and broad brimmed hats, worn by colonists in Australia and the Cape, and the coarse Convict's hat. Besides these we notice an endless variety of children's fancy hats and ladies' hats.

It will be seen from this account that Messrs. Hall & Phillips have not allowed themselves to be distanced by younger competitors. Their business has been extended and developed on all sides; its productive power has been multiplied; the ancient methods of manufacture ha e been improved; the latest achievements of mechanical science have been enlisted in its service; and the most ancient of the Atherstone Hat Manufactories has been kept fully abreast of the resources and requirements of an age of rapid changes and keenest competition.

The Abbey Street premises were largely destroyed by fire in 1967.

Printed in Great Britain
by Amazon.co.uk, Ltd.,
Marston Gate.